HEGEL'S PHILOSOPHY
OF HISTORY

HEGEL'S PHILOSOPHY
OF HISTORY

✢

Burleigh Taylor Wilkins

CORNELL UNIVERSITY PRESS

ITHACA AND LONDON

First published 1974 by Cornell University Press.
Published in the United Kingdom by Cornell University Press Ltd., 2-4 Brook Street, London W1Y 1AA.

International Standard Book Number 0-8014-0819-9
Library of Congress Catalog Card Number 73-16831

Printed in the United States of America by Vail-Ballou Press, Inc.

To Mary Fisher

Contents

Acknowledgments

I wish here to acknowledge an indebtedness to all of Hegel's translators and commentators, especially those commentators with whom I have disagreed the most. The standard of Hegel translation is generally high, and this is especially true in the case of the two translations I have used most frequently: Robert S. Hartman's translation of the Introduction to *The Philosophy of History* and A. V. Miller's translation of the *Science of Logic*. In these circumstances I decided that it would be superfluous for me to attempt to provide alternative translations to ones which were correct and already widely available in English. For not understanding —or dismissing—Hegel too quickly I am indebted to students who have taken the courses in the philosophy of history which I have given at three universities: Princeton, Rice, and the University of California at Santa Barbara. Several friends, including Harold T. Parker and Walter Kaufmann, have read this manuscript, and I am indebted to them for their comments and encouragement. I owe special thanks to the editors of Cornell University Press for the interest they have taken in this project and to the two philosophers who read this manuscript for the Press and made several useful suggestions as to how it might be improved.

BURLEIGH TAYLOR WILKINS

HEGEL'S PHILOSOPHY
OF HISTORY

Introduction

In this interpretative essay I have tried to provide a sympathetic account of Hegel's philosophy of history in the light of Hegel's overall system, with special reference to his *Science of Logic*. I have explored in some detail Hegel's treatment of original, reflective, and philosophical history in an effort to determine what it is that Hegel believed philosophy brings to and learns from the study of history, and I have taken seriously Hegel's claim that philosophical history (the philosophy of history) can answer the question, 'What is the ultimate purpose of the world?' This question and Hegel's answer to it provide the focus of the present essay. From a consideration of Hegel on the relations between non-philosophical history and philosophical history I proceed to examine Hegel's treatment of mechanism and teleology and of contingency and necessity. Hegel argues that mechanism is "sublated" (preserved but gone beyond) in teleology and that teleology provides a more appropriate point of view than does mechanism for the study of history. In the case of contingency and necessity

Hegel maintains that contingency is sublated in necessity and that philosophy is the proper source for a necessitating teleological explanation of the "whole" of human history as a structure aimed at the realization of freedom and self-consciousness on the part of Spirit. From what I have said thus far it should perhaps be clear that I have tried to discuss Hegel's philosophy of history in terms of Hegel's own philosophical problems and that these problems are not always or even usually the problems which contemporary English-speaking philosophers of history are primarily interested in. I believe, however, that contemporary philosophers will see in Hegel's treatment of mechanism and teleology some of their own preoccupations with the problem of explaining human action, and at the end of the essay I venture to compare and contrast briefly Hegel's account of historical explanation with the alternative provided by "the covering-law model of explanation."

In moving back and forth between Hegel's philosophy of history and other aspects of his system I hope that I have at times helped to advance an understanding of his system in the light of his philosophy of history, but my main emphasis has been upon using the system to help explain the philosophy of history. Unlike Hegel, I do not believe the history of philosophy to be necessarily evaluative, but I have nevertheless evaluated, sometimes favorably, sometimes negatively, several of his arguments toward the end of this book. These evaluations, while intended seriously, have been set forth here mainly as heuristics in the task of understanding the main thrust and the significance of Hegel's position, and no systematic or comprehensive evaluation of his philosophy of history has been attempted. I have, however, commented critically upon several interpretations of Hegel's philosophy of history, especially those advanced by W. H. Walsh, Herbert Marcuse, and Karl Popper.

I have not in this short study attempted to assess Hegel's indebtedness to such philosophers as Kant, Leibniz, Spinoza, and Aristotle, or Hegel's influence upon such subsequent philosophers as Marx, the British idealists, or the existentialists. Even within the philosophy of history several important questions remained unexplored: I have not considered Hegel's detailed evaluations in the text of *The Philosophy of History* of the specific ways in which various peoples and cultures have contributed to the development of freedom; such a study would, I think, enrich our understanding of Hegel's historical consciousness, but at this time I believe that a study of the basic philosophical issues discussed by Hegel in the Introduction to *The Philosophy of History* will be more useful. One important philosophical problem posed by Hegel's remarks in the Introduction to *The Philosophy of History* has, however, been neglected here, namely the relation of Hegel's philosophy of history to his moral philosophy; at this point I can only express some doubts as to whether we can, on the basis of what Hegel wrote, answer satisfactorily the question of whether Hegel in effect sacrificed the "autonomy" of moral judgments to considerations concerning our historical situation and "the needs of the time."

Hegel was perhaps the last great systematic philosopher, and he was, I believe, the greatest philosopher of history. But his reputation has not always reflected his achievements, and this has been due in part to a breakdown, following Hegel's death, of a fairly general consensus concerning the proper tasks of philosophy and the emergence of a largely or wholly new set of demands made upon philosophy. Marxists have demanded that philosophy cease trying to understand the world and undertake instead to change it; some pragmatists and existentialists have demanded that philosophy be more responsive to the needs of the individual; and positivists and some ordinary-language philosophers have demanded that philosophers leave off theorizing about phenomena in the world and do conceptual analysis, either of the concepts of science or those of ordinary language. Each of these demands was, intentionally or not, an attack upon Hegel for things he did or did not do. Against this background, the legend or myth has grown that Hegel's philosophy was a tightly deductive system with an almost impenetrable technical vocabulary, and a system in which a dialectic of "thesis-antithesis-synthesis" predominated. According to this legend or myth, everything in the world, even the most minute empirical detail, was held by Hegel to be deducible from his system and explainable in terms of the thesis-antithesis-synthesis formula.[1] Of late, however, Hegel has been treated more fairly: this has been due in large part to the efforts of Walter Kaufmann and J. N. Findlay and in part to the fact that some analytic philosophers now seem disposed to analyze the concepts employed by traditional, systematic philosophers with the same care and rigor they have brought to the concepts of science and ordinary language.

Various editions of *The Philosophy of History*, in German and in translation, have appeared since Hegel's death. Edward Gans' edition of *The Philosophy of History*, based upon Hegel's lecture notes and on notes taken by his students, appeared in 1837. A second, more authoritative edition edited by Hegel's son, Karl Hegel, appeared in 1840, and a third edition edited by Georg Lasson appeared during 1917–1920. The standard English translation by J. Sibree, which was done in 1858, is sometimes cumbersome and inexact; accordingly, I have chosen to use Robert S. Hartman's translation of the Introduction, which appeared in 1953 under the title *Reason in History*. Hartman's translation is based on the Karl Hegel edition but also contains passages from the Gans and Lasson editions, these additions being marked

[1] Gustav E. Mueller, "The Hegel Legend of 'Thesis-Antithesis-Synthesis,'" *The Journal of the History of Ideas*, X (June, 1958), pp. 412–414.

as such by Hartman; it should not be mistaken for a translation of the Introduction in Johannes Hoffmeister's edition, *Die Vernunft in der Geschichte*, which was published in Hamburg in 1955, and which some readers may wish to consult. It should be clear that we are dealing with an impure text and that some caution is called for. I believe, however, that it would be wrong to attach great philosophical significance to differences among the various editions of this text, and in this essay I argue for the consistency of Hegel's *Philosophy of History* with his other works.

CHAPTER ONE

The Varieties of History

Historians and philosophers who are distrustful of the philosophy of history frequently cite Hegel's *Philosophy of History* as a paradigm of what they consider an unwarranted intrusion by a philosopher into the field of historial inquiry. Since the posthumous publication of Hegel's lectures on the philosophy of history the charge that Hegel was "a priori" and "nonempirical" in his treatment of the past has been made repeatedly. It is, however, of more than historical significance that this charge was also made by Hegel—against some of the historians of his day. I shall begin here, hoping that an understanding of what lay behind Hegel's criticisms of the historians of his time will be of some value in deciphering Hegel's philosophy of history.

The Myth of the Historically Given

Near the beginning of the Introduction to *The Philosophy of History* Hegel writes that only the study of world history can show that world history has proceeded rationally and that world history represents the rationally necessary course of the World Spirit; but he cautions us in this same passage that "history itself must be taken as it is; we have to proceed historically, empirically." In the very next sentence, however, Hegel warns that "we must not let ourselves be tempted by the professional historians, for these, particularly the Germans, who possess great authority, practice precisely what they accuse the philosophers of, namely a priori historical fiction." [1] Hegel then gives three examples of such a priori historical fictions: (1) the claim that there was an original primeval people taught immediately by God and possessing a thorough knowledge of all natural laws and spiritual truth; (2) the claim that there were such and such sacerdotal peoples; and (3) the claim that there was a Roman epos from which the Roman historians derived the early annals of Rome.

At this point in the text Hegel adds "and so on" thus indicating that he believes this list of a priori historical fictions could easily be expanded.[2] But the question

[1] *Reason in History* (New York, 1953), p. 12.

[2] The Introduction is not the only place where Hegel quarrels with historians. See, for example, pages 302–303 of the Sibree translation of *The Philosophy of History* (New York, 1944), where Hegel takes issue with Barthold Georg Niebuhr concerning the extent to which the Agrarian Laws of Rome infringed upon the rights of private property: "This discovery of Niebuhr's turns upon a very immaterial distinction, existing perhaps in his ideas, but not in reality." Hegel argues that in regard to the institution of private property Roman ideas were different from those current in Niebuhr's and Hegel's time.

should be raised as to why he has bothered to offer *any* examples of a priori historical fictions on the part of historians. While Hegel's first two examples are complicated by extrahistorical considerations involving questions of religious faith, Hegel must have known that historians have available critical methods and resources *within* their own discipline for the testing of disputed hypotheses—Hegel's third example, being more purely historical, seems in fact to be a paradigm of the kind of hypothesis historical specialists are well equipped to examine critically.[3] It is even more obvious that Hegel was

[3] Hegel's first example is even further complicated, at least for Hegel, by other considerations, as is shown when he returns much later in the Introduction to the question of whether there was an original primeval people. Hegel concedes that the belief that there was such a people and that they possessed an extensive knowledge of spiritual truths has contributed to valuable investigations into man's earliest conditions (he cites the work of Catholic scholars on the history of Oriental religions), but the claim that there was such a people, Hegel argues, remains a supposition which does not and cannot receive historical confirmation. However, Hegel's case against the primeval people hypothesis ultimately hinges not on the questions of evidence and confirmation as these questions are dealt with by historians but upon the question of what are our criteria for considering a given phenomenon to be historical. According to Hegel, the state is a necessary condition of a people's having a history. In the absence of the state the family is pre-historical, and people without a state—even if they have considerable culture—belong to pre-history which Hegel says "lies outside our plan" (*Reason in History*, p. 74). In other words, Hegel finally sees the question not as being one of

not urging us to believe that all or most historical inquiry has as its purpose, or even as an unintended consequence of its labors, the production of fictions, whether
a priori or a posteriori, about the past; nor was he suggesting that the philosophy of history might produce fictions preferable, perhaps on the grounds of their coher-
ence or comprehensiveness, to those fictions produced
by historians. But what then does Hegel's diatribe against
these alleged mistakes by historians accomplish, other
than to suggest to the critical reader that Hegel's invec-
tive masks an uneasy conscience concerning his own intrusion into the historical domain and an awareness on
Hegel's part of how his efforts will be received by historians, an awareness that leads him to strike the first
blow?

What Hegel hoped to bring out in his polemics
emerges more clearly when, following his examples of
a priori historical fictions advanced by historians, he
states as his first condition or postulate that we must
faithfully apprehend the historical. He then notes, however, what he terms "ambiguities" in this postulate. Even
the "average and mediocre historian" who may believe
or pretend that he maintains a simple, receptive attitude
toward his data is by no means passive in his thinking:
"He brings his categories with him and sees the data

---

whether there was in fact such an original primeval people but
of whether their existence was historical in Hegel's special sense
of 'historical.'

through them. In everything that is supposed to be scientific, Reason must be awake and reflection applied." Significantly the very next sentence contains Hegel's dictum, "To him who looks at the world rationally the world looks rationally back." [4] This is followed by Hegel's discussion of Greek and Christian contributions to what Hegel considers the generally shared conviction that Reason rules the world, the Greek contribution being the idea of a scientific law and the Christian contribution being the doctrine of Providence.

Much of what Hegel has been doing in the above is to attack what might best be called the Myth of the Historically Given. The myth that something (direct awareness of physical objects? sense data?) is immediately given to us prior to the intervention of our cognitive faculties has an analog in the area of historical knowledge. The analog is not the claim that we have direct access to the past, for no one, I think, would deny that historians come to know the past through documents, archeological findings, and so on; rather the analog is the belief that the historian must come to historical data or evidence without prior commitments or interpretative categories of any sort—that he must "let the facts speak for themselves." According to this view, the historian should (like "the average and mediocre historian" derided by Hegel) seek to be merely receptive or passive in his attitude toward the data. Hegel's claim is that

[4] *Reason in History*, p. 13.

such a posture is foolish pretense, that everyone, including the most modest historian, necessarily brings categories with him to the data and interprets the data in the light of these categories.

"To him who looks at the world rationally the world looks rationally back" should, however, be read as a warning not to read any variant of historical skepticism into the importance Hegel attaches to the categories which each historian brings to the study of the past. Briefly, the implicit qualification would seem to be this: although each historian necessarily interprets the past by means of a category or set of categories, some categories are better than others. While there is a natural reluctance on our part to think of any of the examples of "a priori historical fictions" cited by Hegel as categories—we would instead speak of them as hypotheses—Hegel's intention, I believe, was for us to see these examples as being the results or consequences of the application to historical data of misleading or inadequate categories and not as simple mistakes of fact or as the results of such simple mistakes. Also, in speaking of how the use or acceptance of such "a priori historical fictions" was quite common among the historians of his day, Hegel suggests a possible connection between the acceptance of such hypotheses and a naïveté concerning the importance of categories to all modes of reflection including the historical. The connection in question, although Hegel doesn't spell this out, seems to be that of vulnerability.

The historian who claims to be merely receptive or passive, who "lets the facts speak for themselves," is especially vulnerable to bad hypotheses or fictions resulting from the uncritical employment of misleading or inadequate categories. (This point is by now a commonplace in historiography, but it was not a commonplace before Hegel.)

Of course, the import of Hegel's remark that the world looks rationally back to the man who looks at the world rationally is not entirely clear, but the sort of thing Hegel had in mind can perhaps be illustrated by the following example. If a natural scientist looks at the world rationally, using appropriate categories and concocting sound hypotheses, a large part of what would count as evidence that the world is looking rationally back upon the scientist in question would be that his predictions concerning the occurrence of certain natural phenomena would prove successful. But what would count as evidence that the world looks rationally back upon the historian, for example, who uses appropriate categories and rejects the hypothesis that there was a Roman epos from which the Roman historians derived the early annals of Rome? And what would count as evidence that the world looks rationally back upon the philosopher who, also using appropriate categories, advances the hypothesis that Reason rules the world? Presumably the kinds of things which we feel would count as evidence would differ significantly for each of these cases, as would our criteria for what constitutes an appropriate category. The relationship between history and philosophy as two modes of inquiry thus remains nearly as mysterious as before. Hegel as much as acknowledges this deficiency when he writes that "we cannot treat here the various modes of reflection, of points of view, of judgment, not even those concerning the relative importance or unimportance of facts—the most elementary category." [5]

In speaking of facts as "the most elementary category" Hegel reveals, if only implicitly, that the position he has been attacking, which conceives of the historian as merely receptive or passive, is not wholly false, for history, when compared with other, more theoretically-oriented disciplines, *is* more responsive to the factual. The danger, Hegel appears to have thought, rests in confusing being responsive with being merely receptive. And this danger has two sides: first, as already noted, there is the seemingly paradoxical risk that an uncritical deference to the factual makes one liable to accept hypotheses which are factually false, as Hegel believed contemporary German historians were wont to do; second, such an uncritical attitude can at best lead only to an attenuated sense of history, such as Hegel found in past Chinese historians: "History among the Chinese comprehends the bare and definite facts, without any opinion or reasoning upon them." Chinese his-

[5] *Reason in History*, p. 13.

toriography, like Chinese science in general, seemed to Hegel to be of a "merely empirical nature." [6]

Hegel's characterization of the facts as the most elementary category is ambiguous in one important respect, for 'elementary' may mean fundamental (and hence necessary) but it may also mean insufficiently sophisticated (not sufficiently reasoned upon). The fact that 'elementary' has these two senses throws some light, I believe, upon Hegel's conception of history. On the one hand, it reveals part of the attraction which the study of history held for Hegel. Hegel's emphasis upon the importance and necessity of mastering the factual may help us understand somewhat better why Hegel became perhaps the finest historian philosophy has produced; more significantly for present purposes, it helps account for Hegel's belief that the philosopher should share the historian's appetite for the factual. On the other hand, the factual is, according to Hegel, severely limited until "reasoned upon." In short, Hegel, as we shall see later in more detail, held that the factual (or empirical) orientation is a necessary but not a sufficient condition for a proper knowledge of the historical process.

The question remains as to exactly what differences Hegel saw between the ways historians and philosophers "reason upon" the facts of history, and this question is complicated by two considerations. Hegel claimed in effect first that historical facts themselves are not so much

[6] *The Philosophy of History*, pp. 135, 134.

given as selected in accordance with various points of view, and second that differences in points of view exist not only between philosophers and historians but among historians themselves—in other words, Hegel believed that a blanket contrasting of historians and philosophers in terms of their approaches to the factual or in terms of some single difference in points of view would be simplistic. Hegel treats the differences among historians' points of view briefly in the first pages of the Introduction, but the significance of Hegel's discussion of the "methods" of writing history is generally overlooked once it is noted that Hegel has here distinguished between original, reflective, and philosophical history. I wish to argue that Hegel in a few pages sketched the outlines of a ladder whereby he believed the historical consciousness could ascend from the nonhistorical (myths, folk songs, and traditions) to a philosophical comprehension of the whole of history, and that in doing this Hegel also gave us a definitive list of the basic *kinds* of points of view adopted by historians. Only when these points of view are compared and contrasted with one another and then with that of the philosophical historian—the philosopher of history—can we adequately understand what it is that Hegel thought philosophy brings to and learns from the study of history. That the significance of Hegel's first few pages is generally overlooked is largely Hegel's own fault. With characteristic modesty he mistakenly thought that his list of the various kinds of nonphilosophical history needed little clarification: "their concept was self-evident." [7]

What might best be termed nonphilosophical or ordinary history is divided by Hegel into "original history" and "reflective history," with "reflective history" being further divided into "universal history," "pragmatic history," "critical history," and "fragmentary history." Like all labels, Hegel's may be somewhat misleading to the uninitiated; thus, for example, while reflective history cannot, as we shall see, also be original history, original history is nevertheless reflective, if only in the ordinary sense of 'reflective.' Herodotus and Thucydides, who are cited by Hegel as authors of original history, obviously reflected upon the events they narrated; and Hegel himself says of the subject matter, the peoples of whom original historians wrote, that such peoples "knew who they were and what they wanted" and proceeds in effect to attribute a comparable self-consciousness to original historians. "Original historians, then, transform the events, actions, and situations present to them into a work of representative thought." [8] Original historians are not reflective historians in Hegel's technical sense, not because they fail to reflect upon historical events but because the events they reflect upon are present to them in a way in which the events dealt with by universal, pragmatic, critical, and fragmentary histo-

[7] *Reason in History*, p. 10.   [8] *Ibid.*, p. 4.

rians are not present to them, and because the objective of original historians is to transform the events present to them into works of *representative* thought: "They primarily described the actions, events, and conditions which they had before their own eyes and whose spirit they shared."[9] Two qualifications in this sentence help to answer the obvious objection to Hegel's characterization of original history, namely that original historians did not as a matter of fact witness all or even most of the actions they described: first, 'primarily' functions much as 'normally' or 'ideally' would, in the sense of indicating the objective or goal that distinguishes one type of inquiry from another; second, the original historians shared in "the spirit" of the actions they described (as Thucydides shared in the spirit of Pericles' character and conduct) and thus they could be faithful to the spirit of actions which they did not actually witness (as Thucydides was probably faithful to the orations of Pericles).

The distinguishing mark of original history is that, of all nonphilosophical or empirical history, it stands the closest to reports of actual perceptions. Hegel speaks of original historians as having "translated the external appearances into inner conception—much as does the poet, who transforms perceptual material into mental images." Yet even here Hegel resists the Myth of the Historically Given. Original historians are considered by Hegel to

[9] *Ibid.*, p. 3.

have been self-conscious, and we know they were usually though not always critical of myth, tradition, and the reports of others; they did not attempt to explain or to describe all that they themselves perceived but instead selected one event, for example, a war or a military campaign, for transformation into "a work of representative thought." Also, since no original historian can perceive a war or a military campaign in its entirety, success in such an undertaking will necessarily depend upon his adoption of an appropriate point of view—and in the case of original history the only appropriate point of view, according to Hegel, is that of a high social position. "Such men must really be of high social position. Only when one stands on high ground can one survey the situation and note every detail, not when one has to peer up from below through a small hole." [10] (Notice the metaphors of perception Hegel uses to convey the advantages of a high social position and the disadvantages of a more humble position, for the original historian.)

Universal history is the first variety of reflective history that Hegel examines. It is, he writes, "the survey of the entire history of a people, a country, or the world." If this is so, one must consider why Hegel has placed universal history at the beginning rather than at the end of his list of the varieties of reflective history— evidently something other than mere comprehensiveness

[10] *Ibid.*, p. 5.

must be involved. The reasons why universal history is to be found at the beginning of the list next to original history rather than at the end next to philosophical history are, I think, several. First, while universal history—like all reflective history—aims at something other than the narration of events that occur more or less within the lifetime of the historian, its basic motive is nevertheless closer to that of original history than are the motives of the other varieties of reflective history. The original historian may have confined himself to a single war or military campaign in the life of a people or country, while the universal historian attempts to be more comprehensive in the facets of a people's life that he attempts to cover or in the length of time in their history which he wishes to span; but in both cases the basic unit of study is the same. It is not an individual or a single institution, but a people or a country as an organized political entity, that usually concerns both the original and the universal historian. To be sure, there are difficulties arising from the universal historian's attempt to take the longer view. He may, Hegel points out, discover that the spirit of his age differs from that of the time about which he is writing. He must also use abridgment and abstraction since the "individual presentations of reality," of original history, are no longer sought.

I should like to suggest that another reason why universal history appears on Hegel's list immediately after original history may be that there is after all no difference in kind between original and universal history but only in degrees of complexity where both the problem of spiritual "distance" between the historian and his subject matter and the problem of selection are concerned. Since Thucydides, for example, was closer "in spirit" to the Athens than to the Sparta of his day, he may have found it more difficult to characterize the motives and actions of the Spartans than those of the Athenians. Such a difficulty, if it existed, is no different in kind from that confronting Livy (whom Hegel cites as a universal historian) when he wrote of the Roman kings and generals of antiquity. Also, just as Livy would speak of a war with the Volsci in a single sentence, so Thucydides, too, practiced the arts of abridgment and selection where the details of the Peloponnesian Wars were concerned. A third reason why Hegel considered universal history before pragmatic, critical, or fragmentary history may be that, just as original history provides raw materials for universal history, so universal history provides raw materials for pragmatic, critical, or fragmentary history.

Let us examine the next variety of reflective history considered by Hegel, the pragmatic. Pragmatic history represents an attempt not only to make the past a part of the present but also, as Hegel's label suggests, to make our heightened awareness of the past useful in solving the moral or practical problems of our day. Although Hegel does not describe it in these terms, pragmatic history represents in part a throwback to original history in the sense that it endeavors to make the past contemporaneous to us. While universal history often serves to remind us of the spiritual distance between the present and the past, pragmatic history represents an attempt to narrow this distance, to quicken stories of the past into present-day life. Significantly, pragmatic history is the first variety of historiography Hegel finds fault with. Whether such history amounts to anything, Hegel observes, depends upon the spirit of the writer; but Hegel argues that we usually find shallow appeals to precedents or analogies such as the appeals to Greek and Roman examples during the French Revolution, while we rarely find the deep insight into situations that makes Montesquieu's *Spirit of the Laws* both "true and interesting." It is in Hegel's reflections on pragmatic history that one finds him saying that "peoples and governments have never yet learned from history, let alone acted according to its lessons," but the usual interpretation of this passage, that Hegel is here condemning peoples and governments for their folly or stupidity, is placed in jeopardy by the very next sentence: "Every age has conditions of its own and is an individual situation; decisions must and can be made only within, and in accordance with, the age itself." [11] Does this mean that Hegel believed pragmatic history is never of any use? I think not,

[11] *Ibid.*, p. 8.

for while Hegel singled out Johannes von Müller's pragmatic history for heavy sarcasm, he praised Montesquieu's as true and interesting and, presumably, useful as
well. The reason why peoples and governments have not
yet learned from history is not simply that every age is
unique, but rather that thus far peoples and governments
have had bad instructors—more von Müllers than Mon-
tesquieus. Also, while each age is unique, there are continuities between ages, and it is our heightened awareness
of these continuities, even when this awareness is fed by
superficial analogies, that accounts for the positive value
Hegel put, although at times begrudgingly, upon pragmatic history. Moreover, pragmatic history represents an
advance in self-consciousness among historians. Hegel
believed that one could only write histories of peoples
who were conscious of themselves (who knew who they
were and what they wanted), and from his scattered
remarks on the qualifications of historians it is evident
that Hegel believed that historians, like the peoples of
whom they write, must also know who they are and
what they want. Pragmatic history with its deliberate
search for resemblances and continuities between past
and present inevitably marks an advance in self-awareness on the part of the pragmatic historian who, more
than the original or universal historian, must come to reflect upon the place of the historian's craft in a wide social context and in relation to matters of public policy.

It is therefore natural that the third variety of reflective history Hegel considers is *critical* history, which is concerned with the history of history and with the critical evaluation of historical narratives. Hegel's previous comparison of von Müller with Montesquieu helps prepare us for the sort of undertaking that is critical history. Here, however, even more so than in his discussion of pragmatic history, Hegel passed out more criticisms than compliments. Hegel believed that critical history predominated among the German historians of his day with what he claimed were unfortunate results: "all kinds of unhistorical monstrosities of pure imagination" are passed off in the name of critical history, and the more historical data are replaced by subjective fancies and the more they contradict "the most definite facts of history," the more wonderful they are held to be by German historians. Hegel wrote, however, that the French by contrast gave us "much that is profound and judicious." So again it is not the variety of history in question that Hegel condemns but what he takes to be instances of its abuse.

The last variety of reflective history is the fragmentary. Hegel has less to say about fragmentary history than about any other kind of history, which is a minor philosophical scandal since it is fragmentary history that provides the crucial transition to philosophical history. Because of the importance of this brief passage and because it is especially terse, even by Hegelian standards, it should be given in its entirety:

The last kind of reflective history is that which presents itself openly as *fragmentary*. It is abstractive but, in adopting universal points of view—for example the history of art, of law, of religion—it forms a transition to philosophical world history. In our time this kind of conceptual history has been particularly developed and emphasized. Such branches of history refer to the whole of a people's history; the question is only whether this total context is made evident or merely shown in external relations. In the latter case they appear as purely accidental peculiarities of a people. But if such reflective history succeeds in presenting general points of view and if these points of view are true, it must be conceded that such histories are more than the merely external thread and order of events and actions, that they are indeed their internal guiding soul. For, like Mercury, the guide of souls, the Idea is in truth the guide of peoples and the world; and the Spirit, its rational and necessary will, guides and always has guided the course of world events. To learn to know it in its office of guidance is our purpose. This brings us to:

3. The third method of history, the *philosophical*.[12]

The above passage reveals Hegel's impatience and haste to arrive at philosophical history. The arrival, however, still requires some explanation. Hegel's metaphors of "external threads" and "guiding soul" and the abrupt

[12] *Ibid.*, pp. 9–10.

introduction of his technical terminology of Idea and Spirit suggest that Hegel perhaps has not thought through carefully, or at least has not explained, how we ascend from the final variety of ordinary historical scholarship to philosophical history. Let us, as a basis for understanding this ascent, begin by briefly comparing fragmentary history with the other varieties of reflective history.

Two varieties of reflective history, the universal and the fragmentary, are explicitly related by Hegel to considerations of a universal nature, and the other two varieties are, I think, also related. Universal history is directly concerned with the universal in the sense that its subject matter is the whole history of a people, a country, or even the world. Pragmatic history is concerned with the universal in the sense of attempting to link the past to the present, by detecting resemblances and continuities between the past and present situations of a people or country (or peoples and countries). Critical history is concerned with the universal, too, if only in the second-order sense of being concerned with the reconstruction of the whole of a people's history by means of a critical study of the history of history. (We might note, too, that critical history, with its concern with the history of history, is a precursor of fragmentary history, which is concerned with the history of art, law, or religion.) Finally, fragmentary history is also concerned with the universal. While fragmentary histories concentrate upon a portion of a people's history they nevertheless "refer to the whole of a people's history," that is to the subject matter of universal history. The principal use Hegel has made of the concept 'universal' in his treatment of reflective history is as a way of talking about the whole, in the sense of a comprehensive history of a people, a country, or even the world. What Hegel has not made clear—and has only hinted at in the sentence where he notes that fragmentary history adopts universal points of view—is that fragmentary history is universal in yet another respect; and thus he has failed to explain why fragmentary history, which "refers to" but does not encompass the whole(s) considered by universal history, is nevertheless the bridge to philosophical history.

An exploration of what Hegel means when he speaks of fragmentary history as adopting universal points of view will, I think, suggest two reasons why Hegel may have placed fragmentary history after universal history and immediately before philosophical history. The first reason is that fragmentary history affords a perspective from which we can better understand why universal history has followed a certain course. Hegel speaks of fragmentary histories as revealing the "internal guiding soul" of historical events. The contrast Hegel draws between "internal guiding soul" and "external thread and order" (sequence) is, I believe, intended partly as a contrast between what does and does not explain historical happenings. Provided fragmentary history is successful, does not in other words make the history of a people's law or religion look like "purely accidental peculiarities" of that people, fragmentary history informs us as to what guides the spirit or consciousness of that people. If one looks at the actual contents of Hegel's *Philosophy of History* and sees the place which the history of law and of religion occupies in his own account of the historical process, one can readily see that Hegel himself frequently used fragmentary history to explain universal history. Here it should be noted that Hegel's use of the word 'fragmentary' as a label for the history of art, law, or religion is at once unfortunate and illuminating, unfortunate because fragmentary history if successful has results which are anything but fragmentary, and illuminating because 'fragmentary' underscores how a part of the whole can explain the content and direction of the whole.

The second reason why Hegel may have placed fragmentary history after universal history and immediately before philosophical history is the importance of the subject matter of fragmentary history from the philosophical point of view. The histories of art, law, and religion are not merely clues to the content and course of history, nor does Hegel mention them as if they were, so to speak, merely accidental examples of fragmentary history. Rather they exhibit the historical development of philosophical truth in prephilosophical forms. Art and religion are limited by the sensuous materials with which they work, and law is limited by the requirements of particular historical situations; but together they provide a means of ascent to philosophical truth—much as fragmentary history provides a means of ascent to philosophical history. I have until now hesitated to employ the technical language of Hegel's overall system, chiefly because I wanted first to see how far one could go in talking about how Hegel conceived of the relationships between the disciplines of history and philosophy without having to take note of the Idea or of Spirit. Even at this point Hegel's claims that the Idea is the guide of peoples and of the world and that Spirit is "its rational and necessary will" are premature in that nothing he has said in his brief discussion of fragmentary history or the other species of reflective history has prepared us to understand or to evaluate these claims—in short Hegel in discussing fragmentary history has leaped into a discussion of philosophical history, which is to occupy the bulk of the Introduction. This move on Hegel's part is, however, more than a sign of haste. More positively, it is a reflection of the close ties uniting law, art, and religion with philosophy. In Hegel's system law stands as an expression of Objective Spirit; and art and religion stand as expressions of Absolute Spirit, ranking just below philosophy and anticipating truths developed more systematically in philosophical inquiry. Thus histories of law, art, and religion are histories of vital aspects of the Spirit, representing developments in time of universal truths.

I shall return to Hegel's conception of Spirit and the Idea, but first I shall finish considering Hegel's outline of the varieties of history. Beginning with pragmatic history and continuing with critical history, Hegel cited what he believed were numerous instances of failure in these modes of historical inquiry. Clearly the possibility of failures occurring in fragmentary history was also in Hegel's mind when he warned of the danger that fragmentary history might reveal only "external relations" between a people's history and the history of their law, art, or religion. But in the event of success, where success means that fragmentary history has shown a people's law, art, or religion to be the "guiding soul" of their actions, what task, if any, remains to philosophical history? To approach the problem from the other direction, original history (if my interpretation is correct) provides raw material for universal history and these two together supply raw material for pragmatic, critical, and fragmentary history, but what is the raw material that any or all of these varieties of ordinary historical investigation can supply to philosophical history? To be sure, they can supply the philosophical historian with an abundance of facts, but at least in the case of *reflective* history these facts have already been reasoned upon. Assuming this reasoning to have been successful, what if anything remains to be done?

That Hegel was aware of these difficulties is evident from his very first remarks in the Introduction concerning philosophical history. The most general definition of the philosophy of history, Hegel writes, would be that it is nothing but the thoughtful contemplation of history; but this reference to thinking, Hegel goes on to say, may appear unsatisfactory. In the study of history, thinking is supposed to be "subordinate to the data of reality, which latter serves as guide and basis for historians. Philosophy, on the other hand, allegedly produces its own ideas out of speculation, without regard to given data." If philosophy came to history with such ideas, it would treat history "as its raw material and not leave it as it is, but shape it in accordance with these ideas, and hence construct it, so to speak, a priori." By contrast the discipline of history is supposed to understand events and actions "merely for what they are and have been, and is the truer the more factual it is." The result of thinking about history and philosophy in this way is, according to Hegel, the claim that there is a "contradiction" between history and philosophy: "This contradiction and the charge subsequently brought against philosophy shall here be examined and refuted." [13]

The problem confronting Hegel at this point hinges in

[13] *Ibid.*, p. 10.

large part upon the metaphor 'raw material' which he has used in his preliminary remarks about philosophical history. I assume that no one has any quarrel with this metaphor when it is used in either of the following ways: first, when we speak of historical documents as raw material for the historian; and second, when we speak, as I have recently done, of how original histories provide raw material for the universal historian. (Here these two ways turn out to be virtually the same, for in the second case original histories become a kind of historical document used by the universal historian.) The metaphor 'raw material' would become troublesome, however, if it were claimed that nonphilosophical or empirical history supplies raw material for philosophical history; here, as Hegel notes above, we would experience a feeling of uneasiness, a fear that philosophy will not leave history "as it is, but shape it" in accordance with philosophical ideas "and hence construct it . . . a priori."

Hegel's difficulty here is a critical one. If my interpretation of Hegel's list of the kinds of history as being not merely taxonomical but hierarchical in intent is correct, then this is the exact spot where Hegel would like to advance the claim that original and reflective histories do in a sense provide the raw material for philosophical history. Before such a claim could be successfully advanced, however, Hegel must dispel the fear that philosophy will proceed to shape and distort this raw material in accordance with its own ideas of what history should be like. The source of this fear, Hegel appears to believe, lies in what might be called our conventional or pre-critical conceptions of history and philosophy, history being conceived of as an effort to understand events and actions "merely for what they are and have been" and philosophy being conceived of as a discipline which produces its own ideas out of speculation without respect for the data in any given area. The charge Hegel thinks he must refute is that philosophy in general and the philosophy of history in particular are a priori in the sense of being indifferent to the way the world really is. Where the conventional conception of history was concerned Hegel evidently felt no need to examine this any further, perhaps because he belived that the limitations of the conventional conception had already been exposed in his seemingly innocent catalogue of the varieties of ordinary historical inquiry.

With the exception of original history (whose aim is the representation, or re-presentation, of events), none of the varieties of history considered by Hegel could be described—assuming Hegel's analyses to have been correct—as being concerned with understanding events and actions "merely for what they are and have been." According to Hegel, their emphasis has been upon treating events and actions as parts of wholes (universal history), as guides to conduct (pragmatic history), as historical constructs obtained from the history of history (critical history), or as explanations—"the guiding soul" —of wholes of which they are a part (fragmentary history). While, however, it might be granted that Hegel has shown the conventional or pre-critical conception of history to be too restrictive, he has not shown it to be false, nor do I believe this to have been his intention. This conception of history needs only to be modified, not abandoned, for the possibility of philosophical history to remain open. The necessary modification is accomplished by underscoring the *reflective* dimensions of historical inquiry, and this Hegel evidently believes he has done by emphasizing the importance of selection, abridgment, construction, and interpretation in non-philosophical histories. Hegel's next task is to show that the conventional or precritical conception of philosophy as being purely speculative is also misleading, and that the belief that philosophy is neglectful of the factual ("the most elementary category") while true of some philosophies is as a general characterization of philosophy simply false. This Hegel has attempted elsewhere; in *The Philosophy of History* he is intent upon demonstrating that *in practice* the philosopher of history can be just as respectful of the facts as is the ordinary, non-philosophical historian—provided, of course, we acknowledge that in neither case are historical facts *given*.

If critical, reflective thinking takes place in both history and philosophy, and if the difference between history and philosophy does not lie between a thinking which is "subordinate to the data of reality" and a thinking that "produces its own ideas out of speculation, without regard to given data," has Hegel in effect denied that there are (philosophically) significant differences between historical and philosophical inquiry? This question is, I hope, rhetorical and useful only as a reminder that what Hegel took to be the real differences between nonphilosophical history and philosophical history still await discovery.

Philosophical History and the Ultimate Purpose of the World

Hegel begins his positive account of what philosophy brings to the study of history with the following remarks: "The sole thought which philosophy brings to the treatment of history is the simple concept of Reason: that Reason is the law of the world and that, therefore, in world history things have come about rationally. This conviction and insight is a pre-supposition of history as such, in philosophy itself it is not presupposed." [14] Through "speculative reflection" philosophy has, according to Hegel, shown that Reason is substance and infinite power, "in itself the infinite material of all natural and spiritual life as well as the infinite form, the actualization of itself as content." Commentators have often concentrated upon problems generated by Hegel's speaking of Reason as substance, infinite power, and in-

[14] *Ibid.*, p. 11.

finite form while neglecting the search for, and the understanding of, the question to which Hegel's claim that "Reason is the law of the world and that, therefore, in world history things have come about rationally" is intended as the answer.

Following his remarks about the powers of Reason, Hegel commences his exploration of the "two aspects of the general conviction that Reason has ruled in the world and in world history." First, he considers the Greek discovery that nature is ruled by universal, unchangeable laws; and second, he examines the Christian belief that the world is "not abandoned to chance and external accident but controlled by Providence." The Greeks, according to Hegel, saw correctly that Reason rules nature; and the Christians saw what the Greeks did not, that Reason also rules the domain of Spirit. Hegel seeks to improve upon the Christian conception of Providence by arguing that we should not rest content with "a retail view" of the nature of Providence but that our faith in Providence should be applied to the whole, "the comprehensive course of world history." It is fashionable, Hegel observes, to admire God's wisdom in animals, plants, and the lives of individual men. "If it is conceded that Providence manifests itself in such objects and materials, why not also in world history?" Hegel denies that the vast scope of world history counts as a decisive objection to this possibility. Hegel at this point considers only one aspect of this objection, whether world history is so vast in scope that God cannot "exercise his wisdom" on so grand a scale. The objection that world history is too large *for us* to know whether God has exercised his wisdom therein is not considered directly by Hegel but has been dismissed in effect somewhat earlier in the text by what is essentially a religious argument: "In the Christian religion God has revealed Himself, which means He has given man to understand what He is, and thus is no longer concealed and secret. With this *possibility* of knowing God the *obligation* to know Him is imposed upon us." [15]

Hegel concludes his remarks on Providence by outlining how he proposes to fulfill the obligation to know God:

Our intellectual striving aims at recognizing that what eternal wisdom *intended* it has actually *accomplished*, dynamically active in the world, both in the realm of nature and that of the spirit. In this respect our method is a theodicy, a justification of God, which Leibniz attempted metaphysically, in his way by undetermined abstract categories. Thus the evil in the world was to be comprehended and the thinking mind reconciled with it. Nowhere, actually, exists a larger challenge to such reconciliation than in world history. This reconciliation can only be attained through the recognition of the positive elements in which that negative element disappears as something subordinate and vanquished. This is possible through the consciousness, on the one hand,

[15] *Ibid.,* p. 16.

of the true ultimate purpose of the world and, on the other hand, of the fact that this purpose has been actualized in the world and that the evil cannot ultimately prevail beside it. But for this end the mere belief in *nous* and providence is not sufficient. "Reason," which is said to govern the world, is as indefinite a term as "Providence." One always speaks of Reason without being able to indicate its definition, its content, which alone would enable us to judge whether something is rational or irrational. What we need is an adequate definition of Reason. Without such definitions we can get no further than mere words.[16]

It is, I think, significant that Hegel in the above quotation claims that the mere belief in *nous* and Providence is not sufficient for the purposes of his theodicy and also that he recognizes that without adequate definition of Reason his own theodicy cannot succeed. Hegel's single remark here about the inadequacy of merely believing in Providence is easily overlooked since it occurs in a passage otherwise so sympathetic to the belief in Providence, but this makes such a remark all the more important, providing as it does some evidence of the unorthodoxy of Hegel's attitudes toward religion, a problem I shall not explore at any length in this essay. Where the issue of methodology is concerned, the above passage may be taken as a warning by Hegel that while his undertaking will be a theodicy like Leibniz's the method will be different. Hegel wrote that Leibniz had

[16] *Ibid.*, pp. 18–19.

proceeded "metaphysically . . . by undetermined abstract categories," and he noted that world history provides the greatest challenge to reconciling the thinking mind to the evil in the world. The contrast between Hegel and Leibniz that emerges from this passage is twofold: first, where Leibniz had proceeded metaphysically, Hegel in *The Philosophy of History* will proceed historically; second, when Hegel uses metaphysical categories in *The Philosophy of History*, these will not be merely abstract and undetermined but will be given an adequate definition. In Hegel's philosophy, as in ordinary language, the opposite of 'abstract' is 'concrete,' and in denying in effect that his categories will be merely abstract and in implying that they will be firmly grounded in world history Hegel is calling attention to the concreteness of the categories he will employ.

We can now approach the question to which Hegel's claim that "Reason is the law of the world and that, therefore, in world history things have come about rationally" is intended as the answer. Hegel writes that "the question of how Reason is determined in itself and what its relation is to the world coincides with the question, *What is the ultimate purpose of the world?*" [17] Hegel believes that this question "implies" that this ultimate purpose (*Endzweck*) is to be "actualized and realized." Accordingly, we must consider both the content of this ultimate purpose and the means of its realiza-

[17] *Ibid.*, p. 20.

tion. Since our present concerns are primarily historio-
graphical, I do not propose to analyze Hegel's detailed
accounts of what various peoples and cultures have actually contributed to the realization of the ultimate purpose
of the world; however, a brief outline of how Hegel
goes about determining the content and the realization
of the ultimate purpose of the world will help us in
marking the difference between the philosophy of
history or philosophical history and nonphilosophical
history as modes of inquiry.

Hegel begins by asserting that world history takes
place within the realm of the Spirit. While physical
nature is important to the world and thus to world
history, "Spirit, and the course of its development, is the
substance of history." The next step is to ascertain the
nature of Spirit—the "nature," "essence," or "substance"
of Spirit, according to Hegel, is freedom. Freedom in
turn is conceived of by Hegel as "its own object of attainment and the sole purpose of Spirit. It is the ultimate
purpose toward which all world history has continually
aimed." [18] The ultimate purpose of the world is freedom,

[18] *Ibid.*, p. 25. In *The Philosophy of Right*, translated by
T. M. Knox (Oxford, 1952), p. 163, Hegel defines Spirit or
Mind as "the nature of human beings *en masse* and their nature
is therefore twofold: (i) at one extreme, explicit individuality
of consciousness and will, and (ii) at the other extreme, universality which knows and wills what is substantive." Hegel's
claim that freedom is the essence of Spirit violates the prejudice
current in some philosophical circles that to speak of the essence
of anything is senseless. For an attack upon this prejudice see

and the means of its realization are the actions and passions of men. But the study of the passions and their consequences presents a melancholy spectacle—Hegel in a well-known passage speaks of the historical process as "the slaughter-bench at which the happiness of peoples, the wisdom of states, and the virtues of individuals have been sacrificed." Hegel asks, "to what principle, to what final purpose, have these monstrous sacrifices been offered?" With this question in mind we can, Hegel claims, make sense out of the seemingly senseless conflicts of individual wills and passions. This can be done by seeing these wills locked in conflict with one another as exhibiting a rationality which is hidden from the agents in question but which is nevertheless furthered by their conflicts. It is in this connection that Hegel speaks of "the cunning of Reason," the main point of this troublesome metaphor being that the passions of historical agents serve to advance or to attain rational ends of which the agents themselves are largely or wholly unaware. The ultimate, in the sense of the most fully rational, end in question is the state which Hegel speaks of as "the realization of Freedom, of the absolute, final purpose." Hegel goes on to affirm that "all the value man

Ruth B. Marcus, "Essential Attribution," *The Journal of Philosophy*, LXVIII (April 8, 1971), p. 202, where essences are defined as "dispositional properties of a very special kind: if an object had such a property and ceased to have it, it would have ceased to exist or it would have changed into something else."

has, all spiritual reality, he has only through the state."
It is in the state that the unity of the universal with
particular wills occurs. In the state freedom achieves objectivity—law is the objectivity of Spirit, and law is
"will in its true form. Only the will that obeys the law
is free, for it obeys itself and, being in itself, is free. Insofar as the state, our country constitutes a community
of existence, and as the subjective will of man subjects
itself to the laws, the antithesis of freedom and necessity
disappears. The rational, like the substantial, is necessary.
We are free when we recognize it as law and follow it
as the substance of our own being." In light of the above
Hegel claims that the state is "the definite object of
world history proper." [19] Earlier Hegel had recognized
that 'state' is ambiguous. It may, he wrote, refer either
to the simple political aspect of a people's life or to the
spiritual content of that life; and he explicitly points out
that he is primarily concerned with 'state' in the second
sense. "For us . . . a people is primarily a spiritual individual. We do not emphasize the external aspects but
concentrate on what has been called the spirit of a
people." [20]

While the question 'What is the ultimate purpose of
the world?' had concerned philosophers of history from

[19] *Ibid.*, p. 53.

[20] *Ibid.*, p. 52. For an excellent criticism of Karl Popper's
interpretation of Hegel as being chiefly concerned with the
political state see Walter Kaufmann's "The Hegel Myth and

St. Augustine onward, Hegel was the last great philosopher of history to believe both that the question itself was fully intelligible and that it could be answered by the philosopher. It was the importance of this question and the incompleteness of all historical investigations which stop short of answering it which, Hegel believed, justified philosophical history or the philosophy of history as a special branch of inquiry. Certainly any question concerning the ultimate purpose of the world seems different in kind from the questions nonphilosophical historians usually ask. Of course, nonphilosophical

---

Its Method," *Hegel's Political Philosophy* (New York, 1970), pp. 137–171. There are, I think, three senses of 'state' in Hegel: (1) 'state' thought of as a political organization, (2) 'state' thought of as a spiritual community, and (3) 'state' thought of as a norm or ideal. What distinguishes Hegel's doctrine is his claim that all actual states—in both senses (1) and (2), I believe —succeed in fulfilling *some* of the requirements of the ideal state: "But if an object, for example the state, *did not correspond at all* to its Idea, that is, if in fact it was not the Idea of the state at all, if its reality did not correspond at all to the Notion [Concept], its soul and its body would have parted; the former would escape into the solitary regions of thought, the latter would have broken up into single individualities. But because the Notion [Concept] of the state so essentially constitutes the nature of these individualities, it is present in them as an urge so powerful that they are impelled to translate it into reality, be it only in the form of external purposiveness, or to put up with it as it is, or else they must needs perish. The worst state, one where reality least corresponds to the Notion [Concept], in so far as it still exists, is still Idea; the individuals still obey a dominant Notion [Concept]" (*Hegel's Science of Logic*, translated by A. V. Miller [London, 1969], pp. 759–760).

historians do sometimes ask questions about purpose, but these questions usually fall into one of two categories. Either they are questions about the purposes, motives, or intentions of particular historical figures or else they are questions about the *functions* of various institutions, practices, pageants, or symbols. But the question of *ultimate* purpose when asked about the whole of human history, or any part therof, is like none of these.

If the question of ultimate purpose is not a question about the purposes of individual agents or groups within the historical process, neither is it a question about the purposes of a Being or God external to the world. In both the *Science of Logic* and the later *Encyclopedia of the Philosophical Sciences* Hegel in his discussions of teleology emphasizes that it is *inner* design which he has in mind when considering the question of ultimate purpose. In the *Science of Logic* Hegel writes that "Where purposiveness is discerned, an intelligence is assumed as its author" but he notes that "The more the teleological principle was linked with the concept of an *extramundane* intelligence and to that extent was favoured by piety, the more it seemed to depart from the true investigation of nature, which aims at cognizing the properties of nature not as extraneous, but as *immanent determinateness* and accepts only such cognition as a valid comprehension." [21] In the *Encyclopedia* Hegel complains that the popular conception of final cause means nothing

[21] *Hegel's Science of Logic*, p. 735.

more than external design. "Teleological observations on things often proceed from a well-meant wish to display the wisdom of God as it is especially revealed in nature" —but Hegel concludes that works written in this spirit do not serve the genuine interests either of science or religion. Design properly understood is, as both Aristotle and Kant saw, best expressed in the idea of *inner design.*[22] In view of the above what Hegel says in *The Philosophy of History* about discovering the plans of God and justifying these plans in a theodicy should not be interpreted as concerning the plans of a God external to the world but rather of a God immanent in the world.[23]

[22] *The Logic of Hegel,* translated from *The Encyclopedia of the Philosophical Sciences* by William Wallace (Oxford, 1892), pp. 346–347, 345.

[23] "Without the world God is not God," Hegel writes in his *Lectures on the Philosophy of Religion,* translated by E. B. Speirs and J. B. Sanderson (New York, 1962), I, p. 200. Although Hegel's philosophy of religion and his conception of the relationship of God and the world, and of God and man, lie largely outside the scope of the present study, two points need noting. First, Hegel, perhaps mistakenly, considered himself to be an orthodox Christian; and he regarded the Christian religion as the highest, and final, embodiment of religious truth. Speaking of the advent of Christianity Hegel affirms: "God is . . . recognized as *Spirit,* only when known as the Triune. This new principle is the axis on which the History of the World turns. This is *the goal* and the *starting point* of History. 'When the fulness of the time was come, God sent his Son,' is the statement of the Bible. This means nothing else than that

In the Introduction to *The Philosophy of History* Hegel uses two metaphors which may prove helpful in understanding his question 'What is the ultimate purpose of the world?'. In explaining how Spirit makes itself actually into what it was potentially, Hegel notes that "the germ bears in itself the whole nature of the tree, the taste and shape of its fruits." Later on he speaks of the building of a house which is, in the first instance, only a subjective design but which, as the house is actu-

self-consciousness had reached the phases of development [*Momente*], whose resultant constitutes the Idea of Spirit, and had come to feel the necessity of comprehending those phases absolutely" (*The Philosophy of History*, p. 319). Second, while it is fashionable and basically correct to speak of the unity of God and man in Hegel's system, Hegel himself cautions against a too facile interpretation of this unity: "But this unity must not be superficially conceived, as if God were only Man, and Man, without further condition, were God. Man, on the contrary, is God only in so far as he annuls the merely Natural and Limited in his Spirit and elevates himself to God. . . . In this Idea of God . . . is to be found the *Reconciliation* that heals the pain and inward suffering of man. For Suffering itself is henceforth recognized as an instrument necessary for producing the unity of man with God. This implicit unity exists in the first place only for the thinking speculative consciousness; but it must also exist for the sensuous, representative consciousness—it must become an object for the World—it must *appear*, and that in the sensuous form appropriate to Spirit, which is the humor. *Christ has appeared*—a Man who is God—God who is Man; and thereby peace and reconciliation have accrued to the World" (*ibid.*, p. 324). In view of the importance of the above my decision not to explore in detail Hegel's philosophy of religion, his analysis of the Trinity and his conception of Christ,

ally constructed, becomes a structure in which the elements are "made use of in accordance with their nature and cooperate for a product by which they become constrained. In a similar way the passions of men satisfy themselves; they develop themselves and their purposes in accordance with their natural destination and produce the edifice of human society." [24] Of these two metaphors the first is in one respect the less informative because while the germ may be spoken of as having an end, the full-grown tree, both the germ and its end belong to the realm of nature and not of Spirit.[25] While nature is related to Spirit its essential relationship is that of subju-

may seem surprising; but besides the practical consideration that one cannot in a short study undertake a definitive project there is a more decisive theoretical consideration. Hegel maintained that philosophy and religion, while having different forms or ways of apprehending the truth, have ultimately the same content (*Lectures on the History of Philosophy*, translated by E. S. Haldane [London, 1892], I, pp. 19–20). If we apply this claim to the study of Hegel's philosophy of history, it could be argued that if we succeed in understanding Hegel's conception of the philosophical significance of history, we will at the same time be understanding, at least substantively, Hegel's conception of its religious significance as well.

[24] *Reason in History*, pp. 23, 35.

[25] Hegel later in the Introduction remarks that "The development of the organism proceeds in an immediate, direct (undialectic), unhindered manner. Nothing can interfere between the concept and its realization, the inherent nature of the germ and the adaptation of its existence to this nature. It is different with Spirit. The transition of its potentiality into actuality is mediated through consciousness and will" (*ibid.*, p. 69).

gation, and since the whole of nature is a means to the end of the development of Spirit, ends found in nature cannot serve as a fully adequate model for understanding an end or ends belonging to the domain of Spirit. In the building of a house, we have the presence of an end—the construction of an artifact to protect man from the elements—and of an intelligence or consciousness—the builder's. But this metaphor is handicapped by two considerations: first, while the elements used in the building of the house "cooperate" according to the laws of their nature they are forced to cooperate by the operations of an *extrinsic* intelligence, that of the builder; second, and more important, the builder knows in advance (on the level of subjective design) both the end of his labor and the means thereto, while in Hegel's system Spirit does not know in advance the means to its self-realization.[26]

While it is doubtful whether any metaphor could in fact provide a fully adequate model for understanding what such a large and complex part of Hegel's system is intended to do, several points about Hegel's question concerning the ultimate purpose of the world and his answer to that question can now be made: (1) Hegel's question refers to purposes or ends intrinsic to the world and its history. (2) These purposes or ends concern

[26] "Only *retrospectively* can Spirit regard the various alien but necessary conditions of its own self-realization as a means to the latter" (J. N. Findlay, *Hegel, A Re-examination* [London, 1958], p. 47).

potentials to be actualized in the world and in world history, but there is no historical inevitability here, any more than there is an historical inevitability that all potential trees will become actual trees or that all potential houses will be built. A germ or a seed may or may not grow into a tree; normally it does, but there is nothing inevitable about it. And despite the obvious differences between Hegel's two examples much the same can be said of designs or plans for houses: designs or plans (as contrasted to wishes or daydreams) are things which we seek to realize in or through action; designs or plans for a house, however, may or may not result in the actual building of a house; normally they do, but there is nothing inevitable about this. The key to understanding Hegel on this point lies in the language of what is *normally* the case and not in the language of either prediction or prophecy.[27] (3) The actualization or realization of these potentials involves a rationality intrinsic to the world, because the potentials to be actualized already possess an essential rationality capable of further growth and development. (4) The actualization of these potentials in such a way as to achieve certain purposes or ends intrinsic to them will involve the use of the materials of nature—and also the passions of human nature—as means thereto. What Spirit ultimately

[27] But see Karl Popper's *Open Society and Its Enemies* (Princeton, 1950), pp. 223–273, and Isaiah Berlin's *Historical Inevitability* (London, 1954), *passim.*

seeks is self-discovery and the actualization, through a struggle with nature and itself, of its own potentials.

Hegel's answer to the question concerning the ultimate purpose of the world involves an interpretation of historical events from a philosophical point of view, an interpretation which Hegel sought to distinguish from interpretations stemming from mere piety or wishful thinking about what the end of history ought to be, as well as from "explanations" provided by the natural sciences. The most difficult problem for Hegel comes, however, from another direction: it has to do with the differences between what philosophical history and non-philosophical history have to say about the past. This problem is the most difficult chiefly because philosophical history and nonphilosophical history are, if Hegel is correct, much closer to start with than are philosophical history and religious piety, wishful thinking, or the natural sciences. Two reasons for the initial closeness of philosophical and nonphilosophical histories are especially noteworthy here. First, Hegel in doing philosophical history has explicitly committed himself to taking history as it is and to sharing that respect for the factual which is characteristic of original and reflective histories; second, philosophical history, original history, and reflective history share a common subject matter, namely Spirit.

Broadly speaking, where the relationship between philosophical and nonphilosophical history is concerned there seem to be two principal possibilities: autonomy and domination. Since original history and the various subdivisions of reflective history are like philosophical history in that each has its own distinctive or characteristic question(s) to put to the past, one might argue that while sharing a common subject matter and a deference to the factual, each variety of history, including the philosophical, divides up this subject matter and selects different facts for emphasis and investigation according to the question(s) it asks. Such an approach to the relationship between the varieties of history will, if pushed far enough, eventually yield these results: the possibility that any variety of history is intrinsically more significant than another will be denied, and the possibility that any variety of history can serve as something more than a heuristic for any other variety of historical inquiry will be rejected. I think that had Kant bothered to draw as elaborate a map of the varieties of history as Hegel has done he would have argued along these lines. Hegel, however, was not a Kantian; and the question to ask of Hegel is in what respects and for what reasons did he view philosophical history as superior and in a sense necessary to nonphilosophical or ordinary history.

Hegel's conception of the relations between philosophical and nonphilosophical history is stated most clearly not at the beginning of the Introduction to *The Philosophy of History* in his treatment of the different kinds of history but in a later section where he attempts

to explain why Spirit's consciousness and development of its freedom must be differentiated into particular national spirits:

That the particular principle of a people is indeed a definite particularity is a point which must be empirically examined and historically proved. This presupposes not only
a practiced faculty of abstraction, but also an intimate ac-
quaintance with the Idea. One has to be familiar, so to
speak, a priori, with the whole sphere of conceptions to
which the principles belong, just as Kepler, to mention the
greatest man in this mode of thinking, must have been ac-
quainted a priori with ellipses, cubes, and squares and their
relations. Only thus, by application of these mathematical
concepts to the empirical data, was he able to invent his immortal laws, which consist in determinations of these concepts. He who is ignorant of the science embracing these
elementary definitions can neither understand nor invent
those laws no matter how long he looks at the sky and the
motions of the stars. This unfamiliarity with the Idea of the
self-development of Freedom gives rise to some of the re-
proaches which are leveled against the philosophical treatment of a supposedly empirical science, in particular against
the so-called a priori method and the introduction of ideas
into the empirical data of history. Such ideas then appear as
something foreign to the material. To a mind which lacks
both knowledge and discipline of thought they certainly
are foreign and beyond the conception which its ignorance
forms of the object. Hence the statement that philosophy
does not understand such sciences. *Philosophy must indeed*

concede that it does not have the kind of understanding which rules in these sciences and does not proceed according to the categories of such understanding. Rather, it follows the categories of Reason. But these enable it to know not only this understanding but also its value and systematic position. It is equally necessary in this procedure of scientific understanding to separate the essential from the unessential and to bring both into relief against each other. To do so, however, one must know the essential; and the essential in world history, seen as a whole, is the consciousness of freedom and the realization of that consciousness in developing itself. The direction toward this category is the direction toward the truly essential.[28]

In the first sentence of this quotation Hegel states "That the particular principle of a people is indeed a definite particularity is a point which must be empirically examined and historically proved," but the remainder of the paragraph seems devoted to showing how little empirical examination and historical proof amount to unless they are informed by philosophical thought and by familiarity with the Idea. To grasp the particular principle of a people one must be familiar a priori with "the whole sphere of conceptions to which the principles belong." Here Hegel has resorted to an analogy with the physical sciences: just as Kepler had to be familiar a priori with the concepts of mathematics and how to apply them to the empirical data in order to be able "to

[28] *Reason in History*, pp. 79–80. My italics.

invent his immortal laws, which consist in determinations of those concepts" so the mastery of the particular principles of various peoples depends upon our ability to master "the whole sphere of conceptions" to which these principles belong and to apply these conceptions to the empirical data of history. If we could not do this, we would be in the position of a physicist without mathematics who could neither understand nor invent the laws of physics "no matter how long he looks at the sky and the motion of the stars." To the objection that the introduction of philosophical concepts into the study of history involves the use of an a priori method and is nonempirical Hegel offers two replies: first, he says in effect that this objection seems well-founded only to a mind which does not think systematically and which consequently is ignorant of the nature of its object, history; second, he admits that philosophy does not have the kind of understanding that one finds in the empirical sciences—nor does it operate according to the categories of such an understanding but instead according to the categories of Reason. The categories of Reason do, however, enable philosophy to "know not only this understanding but also its value and systematic position." Ultimately scientific understanding depends for its success upon its ability to separate the essential from the inessential, and to do this one must know the essential. The essential of world history "seen as a whole" is the consciousness of freedom and the realization of that consciousness in developing itself; here Hegel does not underscore what is to him obvious, namely that it is Reason and not the Understanding, philosophical history and not nonphilosophical history, which can truly comprehend that the consciousness of freedom is the essential aspect of world history.

In glossing the above quotation one might, of course, emphasize Hegel's concessions to the nonphilosophical, empirically oriented study of history or, more correctly in my judgment, one might underscore the limits he detects in such an approach to history. But whichever one does, the two alternative answers of autonomy or domination are too simple where the question of the relationship between the non-philosophical and the philosophical approaches to history is concerned. Either answer is too simple because although Hegel ranks philosophical history above nonphilosophical history the two approaches to the study of history are mutually dependent, much as in Hegel's system Reason and the Understanding are mutually dependent although Reason stands above the Understanding. Perhaps a brief digression into Hegel's views on the relationship between the Understanding and Reason will make this clearer. Hegel's distinction between the Understanding and Reason, while derivative from Kant's, does not depend as Kant's does upon the claim that the categories of the Understanding apply to experience while those of Reason do not. Rather Hegel marked the basic difference between the Understanding and Reason as follows: the categories of Reason, unlike those of the Understanding, have the infinite and the unconditioned as their object. While the categories of the Understanding, being limited to the finite, are not sufficient for philosophical inquiry, they are nevertheless necessary. The Understanding can make clear, precise distinctions without which philosophy would be a vague and merely speculative enterprise; but Reason is necessary to the Understanding as a reminder that the distinctions made by the Understanding are one-sided and incomplete, which is the result of the Understanding's having the finite and the limited as its object.[29]

The application of this brief outline of the relations between the Understanding and Reason to our present inquiry would be as follows. Both nonphilosophical history and philosophical history apply to human experience, nonphilosophical history having past experience or past history as its object, while philosophical history has the whole of human experience, past, present, and future, as its object. However, in order for philosophical history to grasp the whole of human history it must, Hegel believes, first understand that portion of human history which is already past. Original history and the different varieties of reflective history help the philosopher to understand, from different points of view and with the

[29] See Ivan Soll, *An Introduction to Hegel's Metaphysics* (Chicago, 1969), pp. 111–134.

clear distinctions of the Understanding in mind, man's past experiences; such preparation is necessary to the philosopher who seeks to think systematically about the whole of human experience.

At this point, however, it would be easy to become simplistic in one's interpretation of Hegel, chiefly because of difficulties attending the crucial concepts, 'infinite' and 'finite.' One could say that because non-philosophical history is concerned with past experience its subject matter is the finite, the limited, and the conditioned, and that because philosophical history is concerned with the whole of human experience its subject matter is the infinite, the unlimited, and the unconditioned. While it would be correct to say this, it would also on my reading of Hegel be correct to say that non-philosophical history is concerned with the infinite and philosophical history with the finite. Saying both these things would not involve either a contradiction or a denial that there is any difference between the finite and the infinite. It need only involve what Hegel explicitly claims, namely that the relation between the finite and the infinite is *not* a qualitatively distinct relation. Those who think of the distinction between the finite and the infinite as being hard and fast conceive of the infinite in terms of what Hegel calls the "bad" or "false" infinite of the Understanding. The infinite of the Understanding is one of indefinite extension, while the infinite of Reason is thought of by Hegel as being self-contained and complete (though it is not, as J. N. Findlay reminds us, an all-inclusive Spinozistic infinite). According to Hegel, the finite contains the infinite within itself, and the finite when overcome is not transcended by a power outside itself but rather by a power within itself.[30] In his *Lectures on the Philosophy of Religion* Hegel states that Spirit is to begin with finite, and he conceives of this finitude as a necessary part of Spirit's progression toward freedom. "Freedom means to be self-contained, or at home with oneself." To be at home with oneself one must recognize that one's consciousness is both finite and infinite and be aware of the conflict and conciliation between the two dimensions of oneself: "I am not *one* of those taking part in the strife, but I am both the combatants, and am the strife itself. I am the fire and the water which touch each other." [31] The free man is the self-conscious man who, in the name of his infinite consciousness, can criticize and condemn any past or present state of consciousness but who in the act of condemnation and in the effort to advance beyond previous limits reveals his indebtedness to his prior states of consciousness. Since, according to Hegel, history as a form of human inquiry does not commence until man, its subject matter, is in some minimal sense self-conscious (knows who he is and what he wants), history is a

[30] *Hegel's Science of Logic*, pp. 145–146. See also J. N. Findlay, *Hegel, A Re-examination*, pp. 43, 163–164.

[31] *Op. cit.*, I, pp. 59–65.

record of the conflict and conciliation within man of the
finite and the infinite, and this is true of both nonphilosophical and philosophical history. It is also true,
however, that nonphilosophical history is more concerned with the finite and philosophical history more
concerned with the infinite, which helps explain Hegel's
belief that in the final analysis philosophical history is
superior to nonphilosophical history.

Nonphilosophical history has as its object that portion
of human history which is already past; but Hegel insists that not all of the past is merely past: "The moments
which Spirit seems to have left behind, it still possesses
in the depth of its present." [32] Throughout Hegel's reflections on history there is a distinction between those
parts of the past which are dead and those which live on
in the Spirit; this distinction corresponds, I believe, to
Hegel's distinction between those parts of the past which
are accidental and those which are essential to the development and self-realization of the Spirit. What this
amounts to is that nonphilosophical history has under one
conceptualization the finite and the conditioned as its
object but that under another conceptualization its object is the same as that of philosophical history, namely
the Spirit which is infinite and unconditioned. Under the
second conceptualization the principal difference between nonphilosophical history and philosophical history
is that nonphilosophical history elects to consider only

[32] *Reason in History,* p. 95.

past manifestations of this infinite and unconditioned Spirit. Nonphilosophical history helps the philosopher of history to answer the question of how Spirit has developed up to the present time; but nonphilosophical history, while supplying the data for such an answer, cannot give this answer until philosophical history has provided the principles for distinguishing between what is merely finite in the sense of being past and dead (accidental) and what is both finite in the sense of having already manifested itself and yet infinite in the sense of being an essential and hence living element in the development of Spirit.

The reasons why Hegel believed that philosophical history occupies so privileged a position are often misunderstood—and Hegel himself is partly to blame for this. If in the long quotation given above one were to take Hegel's reference to Kepler seriously (as one is entitled, I believe, to take seriously Kant's references to Kepler and Newton in just this connection),[33] one might come to think that Hegel conceived of philosophical history as a fully developed science of human affairs. Hegel's references to mathematical concepts, empirical data, and the laws of physics might then be interpreted in this way: philosophical concepts are to history what mathematical concepts are to physics, the necessary conceptual tools for analyzing empirical data

[33] See my "Teleology in Kant's Philosophy of History," *History and Theory*, V (1966), pp. 172–185.

and for formulating laws covering the behavior of social bodies comparable to those laws we now have for the behavior of physical bodies. Also, there are other passages in Hegel that read as if Hegel were attempting to formulate a theory of social dynamics, one in which struggles and conflicts between individuals and societies proceeding along dialectical lines provide the key to the development of human history. On such an interpretation of Hegel's philosophical history as a fully developed science of human affairs, the theory informing this science would be Hegel's account of Spirit as self-actualizing in time; its concepts would be those of 'Spirit,' 'dialectic,' 'freedom,' 'rationality,' and the like; its "laws" would be something like 'Spirit realizes itself more fully in the passage of time, and more fully in the West than in the East'; and its data would consist of evidence that such and such an event made a certain contribution to Spirit's consciousness of its freedom, and so on.

Not only might Hegel be read this way; historically, I believe, there has been a pronounced tendency to interpret him in this manner. At any rate, many critics have found it noteworthy that Hegel *failed* to satisfy criteria which a fully developed science of human affairs must satisfy. Conceived of in this way Hegel's philosophical history has met with the following objections: its theory is intolerably vague, as are its key concepts; its laws are not laws but at best statements about trends that may persist for a time, but without any guarantee that they will continue to do so; the evidence for Hegel's theory of social dynamics is unimpressive, since with a little ingenuity any event can be made to fit Hegel's theory—indeed the crucial flaw in Hegel's theory is not that it may be used to explain anything but that, given its vague terminology and its confusion of laws with trends, nothing could ever count as falsifying any of its claims. Undoubtedly objections such as these are fatal for some alleged sciences of human affairs, but they are not, I believe, fatal to Hegel who did not in my judgment attempt to provide us with a fully developed science of human affairs, as 'science' is understood today, but rather with a systematic, metaphysical account of man's condition.

One of the essentials of a fully developed science of human affairs would be that such a science would be predictive as well as explanatory, and Hegel's philosophy of history is not predictive. Hegel has very little to say about the future. There are to be sure passages in the text of *The Philosophy of History* where he speaks of fate or destiny, as when he notes that "it is the necessary fate of Asiatic Empires to be subjected to Europeans; and China will, some day or other, be obliged to submit to this fate." [34] Such passages are, however, the exception rather than the rule, and they do not sound much like scientific predictions *or* oracular prophecies. (I shall have more to say later about 'fate' and 'destiny,'

[34] Page 142.

which figure as technical terms in Hegel's *Science of Logic*.) There is also a well-known passage in which Hegel speaks of America as "the land of the future" but this passage, while it falsifies the belief still current in some circles that Hegel thought history would culminate with the achievements of Prussia, actually shows how little Hegel was concerned in his *Philosophy of History* with the future:

It is for America to abandon the ground on which hitherto the History of the World has developed itself. What *has* taken place in the New World up to the present time is only an echo of the Old World—the expression of a foreign life; and as a Land of the Future, it has no interest for us here, for as regards History, our concern must be with that which has been and that which is. In regard to *Philosophy*, on the other hand, we have to do with that which (strictly speaking) is neither past nor future, but with that which *is*, which has an eternal existence—with Reason; and this is quite sufficient to occupy us.

Dismissing then, the New World, and the dreams to which it may give rise, we pass over to the Old World— the scene of the World's History.[35]

This quotation provides a clue as to why Hegel has been misread concerning the position of Prussia in world

[35] *Ibid.*, p. 87. Earlier in his discussion of America Hegel had briefly anticipated Frederick Jackson Turner's frontier hypothesis and also the "safety-valve" aspect of this hypothesis when he noted that in America and especially in the plains of the Mississippi colonization is "constantly and widely open" thus

history, but more importantly it explains why Hegel in *The Philosophy of History* restricts himself for the most part to the treatment of past events. 'History' may refer either to the whole of the past, present, and future or it may refer simply to past and present events (to "that which has been and that which is"). Here Hegel is clearly using 'history' in the second sense, and this limitation helps explain much of the importance which Hegel attaches to Prussia. The particular national spirit of Prussia is already formed while that of America is not, hence he can speak historically (in the second sense) of Prussia but not of America. A second, related reason is that Prussia's achievements in world history can now be compared with the achievements of other nations, while those of America, with its particular national spirit still undefined, cannot. It is not that Hegel thinks that Prussia has actually achieved certain things while America has done nothing (nor that Prussia will no longer continue to achieve various things). Rather Hegel thinks that the achievements of Prussia can be seen as expressions of a particular national spirit while in the case of America this is not yet possible.[36]

---

removing "the chief source of discontent." However, it is consistent with my interpretation of Hegel to recognize that he—or any philosopher—can anticipate or contribute to the development of theories about human behavior without thereby becoming a social scientist.

[36] I am not among those critics who are, in my judgment, unduly concerned over Hegel's alleged belief in the perfection of

It might still be argued, however, that even if Hegel chose to limit himself to a consideration of past and present events, this cannot be regarded as a necessary limitation to philosophical history. To be sure, original and reflective history are necessarily restricted to past and present events, but with philosophical history such a limitation can't hold, for Reason has as its object the infinite, which in this case involves the whole range of human experience including past, present, and future. Thus, Hegel's own characteristic refusal to make predictions about future states of affairs would be due to either (1) false modesty on his part, or (2) a failure to understand the logical force of his own distinctions between

things Prussian and the problems this poses for his philosophy of history. I am, however, concerned over his belief that the Christian religion is "the perfect, absolute religion" and the problems this poses for his philosophy of history. In discussing revealed religion Hegel wrote that "Manifestation, development, and determination or specification do not go on *ad infinitum* and do not cease *accidentally*" (*Lectures on the Philosophy of Religion*, I, pp. 84, 83). From Hegel's claims (*a*) that Christianity is the perfect religion, and (*b*) that the development of religion doesn't go on *ad infinitum* or cease accidentally one might conclude that Hegel believed there would be no religious development, no emergence of new religions to compete with or to replace Christianity, and that he also believed that the historic development of religions stops with Christianity not by historical accident but only by virtue of the perfection of Christianity. If this is what Hegel believed, then it is or ought to be worrisome to students of Hegel's philosophy of history. It must, however, be understood that Hegel's belief in the perfection of

philosophical and nonphilosophical history, or (3) Hegel's tacit recognition that while it was logically open to him as a philosophical historian to make predictions about future states of affairs his system had not developed to the point where in practice he could successfully undertake such a project—Hegel on this interpretation must have understood that his technical vocabulary, consisting of concepts such as 'purpose,' 'inner design,' 'essence,' and 'accident,' simply wasn't up to the standards of rigor and precision required of a predictive science.

Accepting (1) or (2) as explanations of Hegel's reluctance to make predictions would commit us to saying

---

Christianity is not to be confused with an uncritical acceptance of Christianity in any of its finite, institutional forms; rather the perfection of Christianity, according to Hegel, lies in its having revealed the true nature of God and Spirit. But such a belief in the perfection of the Christian revelation is, I submit, consistent with the possible development of new finite forms of religion which may ignore, misinterpret, or deny this revelation. It is also consistent with the possibility that the development of religion might as a matter of historical fact have stopped short before the advent of Christianity or the proper comprehension of the Christian religion. (Hegel himself believed that the proper comprehension of Christianity had had to wait until the Protestant Reformation, and it could be argued that the non-occurrence of the Protestant Reformation was at some time a genuine historical possibility.) If the above is correct, Hegel's claim that the development of religion doesn't go on *ad infinitum* or cease accidentally would now require restatement either in the language of what will "normally" be

that Hegel didn't understand his own system or its consequences; accepting (3) would commit us to saying that Hegel understood all too well that what he had in effect claimed to be logically open to the philosophy of history was not a real possibility for his own particular philosophy of history. Accepting (1) or (2) would, I think, be a sign of desperation, an admission of a possible failure to understand Hegel; (3) by contrast has a certain initial attraction. The strength of (3) is that it seems to acknowledge that, provided Hegel had made revisions in his system (including the use of a somewhat different set of concepts), Hegel's own philosophy of history could have moved toward becoming a fully developed predictive science of human affairs, with Reason build-

---

the case or else with some "other things being equal" qualification. Such a qualification would allow us to say that to the extent that man actualizes his potentials for rational development and to the extent that he is able to comprehend correctly the significance of revealed religion, he will not allow either the needless proliferation of religions or a premature cessation of religious development. And this need not in any way commit Hegel to claims about what finite, historical forms religion may or may not take at some future time. In short there may be religions and hence histories of religions after Christianity; all that Hegel need claim is that such religions will necessarily be a falling away from the rational perfection of the Christian revelation.

I believe that an argument similar to the above could be constructed in reply to those who are of the opinion that Hegel's alleged belief in the political perfection of Prussia

ing upon and systematizing the findings of the Understanding. But the weakness of (3) is that it implies that Hegel's failure to move in this direction was literally a failure, brought about in part because of certain inadequacies in the technical vocabulary he employed. We can, I think, find two more adequate reasons why in Hegel's hands the philosophy of history did not move toward becoming a predictive science: one, Hegel's conception of philosophical inquiry had, as we shall see, an essentially retrospective cast; and two, while it is true that Hegel's technical vocabulary wasn't up to the tasks required of a fully developed predictive science of human affairs this shows not that Hegel was a Moses destined to glimpse but not to enter the Promised Land of Predictive Science but that his intention was to go elsewhere.

In contrasting philosophy with history Hegel notes that philosophy is concerned with "that which (strictly speaking) is neither past nor future, but with that which is, which has an eternal existence—with Reason." In other words, the differences in *tense* which are so important to the nonphilosophical historian and to the man in the street lose much of their significance to the philosopher who has the eternal as the object of his inquiry. But

---

somehow implies the further belief on his part that certain future political developments or certain kinds of political developments are thereby rendered impossible; but I shall not attempt to develop such an argument here, mainly because it is fairly obvious how the argument would proceed.

if in Hegel's system philosophical inquiry has this time-
less dimension it has also a decidedly temporal aspect:
first, there is Hegel's determination to find signs or evidence of the eternal "is" in the temporal "is" and "was"
of present and past events, which accounts for much of
Hegel's interest in history; and second, Hegel conceives
of philosophical inquiry as being to a large extent retrospective, a recapturing of the past (including especially
the history of philosophical thought) rather than an an-
ticipation of the future. In the Preface to *The Philosophy
of Right* Hegel remarks that philosophy always comes on
the scene too late to give instruction as to what the world
ought to be, and in elaborating upon this point Hegel
goes beyond moral philosophy to provide an essentially
retrospective picture of the relation of *all* modes of
philosophy to reality:

One word more about giving instruction as to what the
world ought to be. Philosophy in any case always comes on
the scene too late to give it. As the thought of the world,
it appears only when actuality is already there cut and dried
after its process of formation has been completed. The
teaching of the concept, which is also history's inescapable
lesson, is that it is only when actuality is mature that the
ideal first appears over against the real and that the ideal apprehends this same real world in its substance and builds it
up for itself in the shape of an intellectual realm. When
philosophy paints its grey in grey, then has a shape of life
grown old. By philosophy's grey in grey it cannot be re-

juvenated but only understood. The owl of Minerva spreads its wings only with the falling of the dusk.[37]

It is not difficult to establish that Hegel conceived of philosophy as having a retrospective rather than a prospective point of view; it is more difficult to understand why he believed philosophy to be limited in this way. Here it may be helpful to consider the context of moral philosophy in which the above quotation occurs even though the point Hegel makes is by no means restricted to that context. Like most conservatives, Hegel was profoundly impressed by the ways in which reality may prevent or significantly alter the implementation of our subjective ideals; in *The Philosophy of Right* shortly before the famous "owl of Minerva" passage he derided Plato for recommending that nurses move about with babies and rock them continuously in their arms and Fichte for suggesting that suspects not merely sign their passports but have their likenesses painted on them. This kind of detailed recommendation as to how the world ought to be was, Hegel believed, unsuited to the task of philosophy. It is only when "actuality is mature" that the ideal (as opposed to *mere* ideas) emerges with sufficient clarity for the philosopher to understand it. "When philosophy paints its grey in grey, then has a shape of life

[37] *Hegel's Philosophy of Right*, translated by T. M. Knox (Oxford, 1952), pp. 12–13. See also *Hegel's Lectures on the History of Philosophy*, I, p. 52.

grown old" is not, however, a counsel of despair, even if the image of philosophy painting its grey in grey may seem somewhat unflattering to the philosopher. "A shape of life grown old" is a shape of life which has matured enough for us to understand which of its potentials it has actualized and to grasp the rationale of its institutions and practices. The philosopher cannot teach the state how it ought to be, but it can "show how the state, the ethical universe, is to be understood" and it can also provide a reconciliation between "reason as self-conscious mind and reason as an actual world before our eyes" by showing us the rationality in the world in which we live. "To recognize reason as the rose in the cross of the present and thereby to enjoy the present, this is the rational insight which reconciles us to the actual." Which is not to deny that the present has its burdens, its crosses, but rather to affirm that there is "less chill in the peace with the world which knowledge supplies." [38] To look at the world retrospectively is to understand how we have come to be where we are and, according to Hegel, there is always an intellectual joy in such an understanding which cannot be annulled by the further discovery that where we are is much less than perfect. Finally, if we knew exactly how Spirit could become fully self-conscious and free, then we would know how to go about altering present, imperfect reality to

[38] *Hegel's Philosophy of Right*, p. 12.

achieve this end; but an important feature of Hegel's teleology is the claim that while we can know the ultimate purpose of the world we cannot know in advance the particular ways or means whereby this purpose will be realized. Only in retrospect, historically, is such detailed knowledge possible.

CHAPTER TWO

Mechanism and Teleology

Hegel, I have maintained, was not interested in making either conditional predictions or unconditional prophecies about future events. Instead his interest lay in posing and answering the question, What is the ultimate purpose of the world? I have been concerned with this question as it occurs in Hegel's philosophy of history, but it is fully intelligible only in the context of Hegel's overall system and more specifically in the context of Hegel's discussions of the principle of teleology as these occur in the *Science of Logic* and the *Encyclopedia*. I wish now to examine these discussions.

How Mechanism Is "Sublated" in Teleology

Hegel's conception of the principle of teleology is revealed to a considerable extent in his criticisms of Kant's treatment of the Ideas of Reason. In Kant's hands, Hegel complains, Reason becomes a "wholly formal, merely regulative unity of the systematic employment of the understanding" and the Ideas of Reason do not "possess a constitutive character as do the categories; they are *mere* Ideas" which we are to understand as being nothing more than hypotheses. Kant's reason for conceiving of the Ideas of Reason as regulative rather than constitutive is, Hegel writes, that they "*do not* occur in any experience." In a tone compounded of wonder and sarcasm Hegel then asks, "Would one ever have thought that philosophy would deny truth to intelligible entities because they lack the spatial and temporal material of the sensuous world?" [1] In short, Hegel denies that the Ideas of Reason are merely regulative, or merely hypotheses, or merely ways of looking at the facts of human experience or at the world.

In treating Kant's views on the Idea of Reason with which we are here concerned, the principle of teleology, Hegel is more respectful. He speaks of Kant's distinction between relative or external and internal purposiveness as "one of Kant's great services to philosophy." In

[1] *Hegel's Science of Logic*, p. 590. Behind Kant's failure to recognize the constitutive character of the Ideas of Reason there lay, Hegel believed, a more pervasive failure to grasp the relation of thought to sensuous reality, this failure being evident in Kant's belief that thought apprehends the world of appearance and not reality, not the thing-in-itself. However, Hegel's criticism of Kant's doctrine of the thing-in-itself lies outside the scope of this study. Here we need only note Hegel's insistence that, in the light of Kant's claim that we cannot know the thing-in-itself, even those categories which Kant believed to be constitutive can be for Kant constitutive only of the world of appearance.

his treatment of internal purposiveness Kant, according to Hegel, has opened up the concept of life, the Idea, and "has done *positively* for philosophy what the *Critique of Reason* did but imperfectly, equivocally, and only negatively, namely, raised it above the determinations of reflection and the relative world of metaphysics." [2] Hegel's conception of the relationship between internal purposiveness and the Idea will be discussed later, but here despite Hegel's praise for what Kant has done it is Hegel's criticism of Kant for what he has failed to do that is the more important. What Kant has failed to do, according to Hegel, is to answer "the sole question to which philosophic interest demands an answer," namely which of two principles, the principle of teleology or the principle of mechanism, "possesses truth in and for itself." Hegel complains that both principles must, if Kant is correct, be regarded not as "objective propositions" but as "subjective maxims" or ways of looking at the world. As the occasion warrants one can look at the world from the point of view of teleology or from the point of view of mechanism; but one cannot, if Kant is correct, decide as to the truth of these points of view.[3]

The importance Hegel attached to the question of teleology versus mechanism was to a considerable extent a function of his belief that larger issues were involved here. Hegel regarded the opposition of teleology and

[2] *Ibid.*, p. 737.   [3] *Ibid.*, pp. 738–739.

mechanism as an instance of "the more general opposition of *freedom* and *necessity*" [4]; and Hegel also saw in the ascendancy of teleology over mechanism the crucial step toward the absolute unity of the Concept (*Begriff*) and the Idea (*Idee*). Where the first of these issues is concerned Hegel follows Kant quite closely. Hegel writes that Kant has exhibited the opposition of freedom and necessity in *The Critique of Pure Reason* in his treatment of the antinomies of reason, as the third conflict of the transcendental ideas, and again in his *Critique of Teleological Judgment*. The thesis of the third antinomy is that causality according to natural laws is not the sole causality from which the phenomena of the world can all be derived, and thus a causality through freedom must also be assumed. The antithesis of the third antinomy is that there is no freedom but everything in the world happens solely according to natural laws. According to Hegel, however, Kant's treatment of this antinomy is needlessly roundabout. All that is essentially involved, Hegel believed, is the following: in order to prove the thesis we have to assume that there is no causality other than that which takes place according to natural laws—the necessity of mechanism in general—but this proposition is self-contradictory because we take natural law to consist in that nothing happens without a cause sufficiently determined a priori, which cause therefore must contain an absolute spontaneity within itself; that is, the

[4] *Ibid.*, p. 737.

assumption opposed to the thesis cannot be made because it contradicts the thesis. In the case of the antithesis basically the same sort of difficulty confronts us, for here to prove the antithesis we must assume that there exists a freedom, as a particular kind of causality, that absolutely initiates a state of things and the consequences of that state. But such a beginning presupposes a state that has no causal connection with its predecessor and this contradicts the law of causality which alone makes the unity of experience and experience itself possible. The assumption of freedom, which is opposed to the antithesis, cannot be made because it contradicts the antithesis. Hegel notes that the same antinomy recurs in Kant's *Critique of Teleological Judgment* where Kant treats the opposition between the assertion that all production of material things takes place according to merely mechanical laws and the assertion that some cases of production of material things according to such laws are not possible.[5]

The relationship in Hegel's system of the problem of teleology and mechanism to the larger issue of the unity of the Concept and the Idea is, if anything, even more complex. Those passages in the *Science of Logic* and the *Encyclopedia* where Hegel tries to show that teleology is superior to mechanism and that the ascendancy of teleology over mechanism makes possible the unity of the Concept with the Idea are among the most difficult passages in Hegel, hard to follow in their detail and impos-

[5] *Ibid.*, pp. 737–738.

sible to summarize adequately in a few pages. However, with our interest in Hegel's philosophy of history as the occasion for our interest in Hegel's treatment of teleology and mechanism, we can perhaps afford to be more selective than would otherwise be warranted.

Hegel's solution to the problem of teleology and mechanism, stated summarily, is that mechanism is "sublated" in teleology. Hegel maintained not that teleology and mechanism are two opposed points of view the truth of which is undecidable, but that on different levels teleology and mechanism are both true; however, the truth of teleology is more complete, incorporating into itself the truth of mechanism while overcoming its limitations. The metaphor of "levels" should, however, be handled with caution, for in one important sense teleology and mechanism occur on the same level, namely that of objectivity, the in-and-for selfness of the Concept. Objectivity in this sense, however, is not attainable all at once; rather it must pass through stages, which are represented by three categories: mechanism, chemism, and teleology. However, as these stages represent ascent or progress toward a higher objectivity, the metaphor of "levels" remains appropriate.

Of course, what has traditionally been regarded as the ultimate question about "levels" and categories goes beyond Hegel's account of teleology and mechanism to concern the whole of his system. Basically it has to do with whether the relations between the categories in Hegel's system are logical or temporal. Are the categories antecedent to nature and history? Is the antecedence only a logical and not a temporal one? Do the categories have no existence apart from the world of experience? These are the questions which separated Right and Left Hegelians and which continue to divide Hegel scholars. It may be, as Alasdair MacIntyre has suggested, that Hegel was genuinely ambiguous concerning these questions,[6] in which case one has a license of sorts to paint one's picture of Hegel as one pleases. A more exciting possibility, however, is that if the teleological approach holds the key not just to Hegel's philosophy of history but to his entire system, the significance attached to these questions will largely disappear. Such questions rest ultimately upon a distinction between logical and temporal which loses much of its relevance before a world-view in which immanent purposiveness reigns supreme. Here the world is seen as struggling in time to manifest a purposiveness already implicit in it; and logic as the study of the categories by which we interpret the world tells us that one category, that of purposiveness, will prove more adequate to our interpreting the world than others, not in terms of some pragmatic notion of adequacy but by virtue of the ontological superiority of this category to others we use. Whether the

[6] *Herbert Marcuse* (New York, 1970), p. 31.

teleological interpretation of Hegel's entire system will work lies outside the range of this study; it can, however, be shown that it does work as a key to understanding Hegel's treatment of objectivity in his *Science of Logic*.

Hegel writes that mechanism "the first form of objectivity is also the category which primarily offers itself to reflection, as it examines the objective world. It is also the category beyond which reflection seldom goes." [7] Hegel does not believe, as one might initially suppose, that mechanism is limited in its application solely to the realm of nature; he calls our attention to the presence in ordinary language of locutions such as 'a mechanical style of thinking,' 'a mechanical memory,' 'habit,' and 'a mechanical way of acting' in support of his claim that mechanism is applicable to some aspects of the life of the Spirit. Hegel maintains, however, that a critical scrutiny of the use of these locutions will show how limited the category of mechanism is in the realm of the Spirit. In those cases where we use the category of mechanism the distinguishing characteristic of Spirit, the freedom of individuality, is lacking in what Spirit does.[8] Even in its application to the world of nature mechanism is, according to Hegel, severely limited. He describes it at one point as "a shallow and superficial mode of observation, one that cannot carry us through in connection

[7] *The Logic of Hegel*, p. 337.
[8] *Hegel's Science of Logic*, p. 711.

with Nature and still less in connection with the world of Mind. In Nature it is only the veriest abstract relations of matter in its inert masses which obey the law of mechanism." [9]

Hegel was no more diffident about involving himself in what we would be inclined to consider as strictly scientific issues than he was in taking issue with the historians of his day. He maintained that physical phenomena such as light, heat, magnetism, and electricity cannot be explained in terms of mechanical processes such as "pressure, impact, displacement of parts, and the like." Phenomena such as the growth and nourishment of plants and perhaps animal sensations as well are even more immune to explanation along these lines. Hegel writes, "It is at any rate a very deep-seated, and perhaps the main, defect of modern researches into nature, that, even where other and higher categories than those of mere mechanism are in operation, they still stick obstinately to the mechanical laws; although they thus conflict with the testimony of unbiased perception, and foreclose the gate to an adequate knowledge of nature." [10]

Hegel uses 'mechanism' for two different purposes: first, he uses it to report what he takes to be the results of the mechanical sciences of his time, and second, he uses it to describe a distinct world-view which he compares and contrasts with another world-view, that of teleology. His use of 'chemism' is affected by a similar

[9] *The Logic of Hegel,* p. 337.   [10] *Ibid.*

duality of purpose, with the result that commentators are frequently uncertain as to how Hegel's discussions of mechanism and chemism should be interpreted; it is with some relief that they move on to Hegel's treatment of teleology, the philosophical significance of which is more readily apparent. Yet in a way this difficulty is an artificial one which shows chiefly that our conception of the task of philosophy has become a great deal narrower than was Hegel's. Hegel's treatment of mechanism should, I think, be read as consisting of three stages: (1) he attempts to understand the achievements of the mechanical sciences of his time, and he finds that their successes have been largely in accounting for the highly abstract relations of matter in its inert masses; (2) he claims to have found that the mechanical sciences are less successful in dealing with other physical phenomena and largely unsuccessful in dealing with spiritual phenomena; and (3) he explains the successes and failures of the mechanical sciences as being due to their conception of the objects of scientific inquiry, and he argues that while their conception is adequate for certain very restricted purposes it is woefully inadequate for other purposes. The third stage of Hegel's treatment of mechanism involves an analysis of what, in rather more modern language, is sometimes called the metaphysical presuppositions of the empirical sciences. By the time this task is done an entire world-view has been outlined, for the question of how we conceive of the objects of inquiry involves other questions—for example, the question of how we conceptualize the actions and reactions of the objects in question upon one another. On this interpretation of what Hegel is doing, Hegel ultimately thinks of the mechanical sciences as applications to the world of a certain worldview or perspective and as a test of sorts for the adequacy of this way of looking at the world.

If this is in fact what Hegel is doing in his treatment of mechanism, then he is vulnerable to a number of fairly obvious objections. Insofar as he argues not merely that the mechanical sciences do not but that they cannot explain certain phenomena he is, of course, open to the charges of dogmatism and apriorism which so often accompany his excursions into science.[11] To such charges Hegel might conceivably reply that he, like Aristotle, conceives of a science in part in terms of whether its methodology is appropriate to the phenomena with which it seeks to wrestle, and that it is not clear that one can never say that some methodologies are so glaringly inappropriate to certain kinds of phenomena that failure in their application is virtually guaranteed. I think that the more interesting objections to what Hegel is doing in his treatment of mechanism concern whether his account

[11] Hegel's critics accuse him of having offered in his inaugural dissertation *On the Orbit of the Planets* a deductive argument to the effect that no planet could be located between Mars and Jupiter. See Walter Kaufmann, *Hegel* (Garden City, 1965), pp. 76–79, for a clarification of what Hegel actually did say on this matter.

of the metaphysical presuppositions of the mechanical sciences is correct and whether his explanation of the successes and failures of the mechanical sciences in terms of these metaphysical presuppositions is also correct— mightn't it turn out to be the case that an explanation of success and failure in terms of developments wholly *within* the mechanical sciences is after all the correct explanation? I doubt, however, whether satisfactory answers to these questions will be forthcoming: Hegel, rather typically, does not provide a detailed analysis of the positions he is discussing; and as a consequence the exact nature of the relationships he saw as obtaining between the mechanical sciences and their presuppositions isn't spelled out. Fortunately for our purposes, the answers to these questions can wait; here we need only to determine what Hegel believes mechanism, conceived of as a world-view, has to say about objects and their relations with one another and what Hegel thinks are the limitations of mechanism in this regard.

Hegel writes that the object, mechanistically conceived, does not differentiate itself into matter and form and has neither properties nor accidents. The object conceived of in this way is indeterminate and immediate, and yet its being is determined. The determinateness of its totality lies outside it in other objects and these in turn have the determinateness of their totality outside them, and so on. Mechanism, according to Hegel, seeks to preserve the distinctness of objects and yet ends up conceiving of objects as entirely determined by one another. In denying that objects have an essential nature (Hegel doesn't use this phrase here but this is what is involved in his remarks about matter and form, property and accident), mechanism conceives of objects as being indifferent both to their being determined and to their active determining. Mechanism involves, Hegel maintains, "a manifest contradiction between the complete mutual *indifference* of the objects and the *identity* of their *determinateness*, or the contradiction of their complete *externality* in the *identity* of their determinateness. This contradiction is, therefore, the *negative unity* of a number of objects which in that unity, simply repel one another: this is the mechanical process." [12] We need not concern ourselves here with whether it actually is contradictory, as Hegel claims, to affirm both that objects are mutually indifferent and that they are nevertheless identical in their determinateness, for the main thrust of Hegel's argument against mechanism is that its claim that objects are mutually indifferent is false. In fact Hegel argues, appealing in part to the findings of chemistry, objects do exhibit an attraction toward one another; moreover, it is the case that objects have a tendency toward self-organization and self-determination.

When we speak of mechanism as being blind this involves, Hegel notes, what is called fate; and in his remarks about fate one can find significant evidence con-

[12] *Hegel's Science of Logic*, p. 714.

cerning what Hegel takes to be true and false in mechanism. Hegel remarks that "mere objects, merely animate natures, like all other things of a lower grade, have no fate" for what happens to them is contingent and external; or to put it somewhat differently, mere objects have as their immediate nature contingency and externality, meaning that they are the sorts of things whose fate is determined contingently rather than necessarily and by objects external to them. So much for blind fate; fate proper is different: "Only self-consciousness has a fate in the proper meaning of the word, because it is free, and therefore in the individuality of its ego possesses a being that is absolutely *in and for itself* and can oppose itself to its objective universality and estrange itself from it. By this very separation, however, it excites against itself the mechanical relationship of a fate. In order therefore that this fate should be able to have power over it, it must have given itself some determinateness or other conflicting with the essential universality; it must have committed a *deed*." By becoming estranged from its essence, the subject becomes an object and takes on the relationship of externality toward its essential nature, and it is this relationship which makes it an object which can be thought of in the terms of mechanism. Both the fate of mere objects and the fate of self-consciousness involve the external; but while the external can be said to be the immediate nature of mere objects (their only essential nature is that their fate is shaped for them by objects or forces outside themselves), externality figures differently in the case of self-consciousness which seeks, as Hegel puts it elsewhere, to hide itself from itself. It is by its own activity that self-consciousness is externalized; self-consciousness differs from mere objects in that it possesses an essential nature from which it seeks to escape. The fate of self-consciousness is "a fate immanently determined and rational—a universality that *particularizes itself from within*, the difference that is at rest and is constant in the unstable particularity of objects and in their process; in other words, the law. This result is the truth, and therefore also the foundation, of the mechanical process." [13]

Hegel concludes his account of mechanism by making a distinction between what he calls dead mechanism and free mechanism. Dead mechanism is the mechanical process wherein objects appear to be self-subsistent but actually have their "centre outside themselves; this process exhibits either contingency and indeterminate dissimilarity or formal unity." Such a uniformity, Hegel writes, is indeed a rule but not strictly speaking a law. Only free mechanism actually has a law, which Hegel calls "the spontaneous determination" of pure individuality or of the explicated concept: "As difference it is in its own self the imperishable source of self-kindling movement, and since in the ideality of its difference it related itself to it-

[13] *Ibid.*, pp. 721–722.

self alone, it is free necessity." [14] In the movement from dead mechanism to free mechanism the transition away from mechanism is at hand, for free mechanism, according to Hegel, determines itself into chemism.

An object as conceived of by mechanism is a totality indifferent to determinateness, but an object as conceived of by chemism is significantly different. Here its determinateness, its relations to other objects, and the kind and manner of this relationship, "belongs to its nature." What Hegel calls chemical objects—and these are not limited to the objects studied by chemistry but include such things as the sex relation—exhibit a lack of indifference and the presence of a strong attraction or bias toward one another. They strive to overcome their apartness and to become one in their existence. The product of the chemical process, according to Hegel, is "the neutral object" in which the properties of the chemical objects which come together are merged, but this neutral product may disintegrate and the objects which merged together in it may pass back into separate (but now indifferent and not merely different) existences. But whether it is union or disintegration that marks the chemical process, the chemical object is not wholly self-determining; external conditions are required if chemical elements are

[14] *Ibid.*, p. 725. Some of the difficulty attending Hegel's attempts at reconciling freedom and necessity is diminished if we attend to an earlier statement in this work: "Necessity does not become freedom by vanishing, but only because its still inner identity is manifested" (*ibid.*, p. 571).

to come together or become separate. What Hegel is saying here is that the built-in biases of chemical objects constitute a necessary but not a sufficient condition for their interacting as they do, and chemical objects ultimately partake of the same deficiency—dependence upon external factors—which characterizes mechanical objects. A further advance beyond "externality" and "conditionedness" is needed, and this is provided by the third stage of objectivity, teleology, in which the Concept of the end makes its appearance.[15]

In his discussion of teleology Hegel several times remarks that "the end" or "the end relation" is the truth of mechanism, which is here taken to include chemism also. By this he intends, I believe, to advance two separate but related claims: first, he wishes to claim that teleology possesses "a higher principle" than does mechanism; and second, he wishes to claim that the means-end relation of teleology utilizes the cause-effect relation of mechanism. The higher principle possessed by teleology is that of the Concept in its existence, "which is in and for itself the infinite and the absolute—a principle of freedom that in the utter certainty of its self-determination is absolutely liberated from the *external determining* of mechanism." [16] But if in mechanism the Concept is unfree and submerged in externality and if in teleology the Concept is free and self-determining, why does Hegel speak of the end or

[15] *Ibid.*, pp. 727–733; *The Logic of Hegel*, pp. 341–343.
[16] *Hegel's Science of Logic*, p. 737.

the end relation as the *truth* of mechanism instead of saying simply that mechanism is false and that teleology is
true? One major reason for this, I believe, is that Hegel
saw the truth of teleology as developing out of positions
identified with mechanism and chemism: hence his refusal to treat the positions identified with mechanism and
chemism as mere or simple errors, a refusal which was in
accord with Hegel's overall reluctance to look upon any
philosophical position as a mere or simple error.[17]

In mechanism the Concept does not exist in the object,
since the object is not self-determining; in chemism the
Concept has either a one-sided existence in a state of ten-
sion or else is external to itself [18]; in teleology the Concept which was "present only in the germ" in mechanism
and chemism is liberated and the Concept "in the shape
of the aim or end thus comes into independent exis-

[17] Hegel writes in the Preface to the *Phenomenology* that
philosophical truth "includes the negative as well—that which
might be called the false if it could be considered as something
from which one should abstract. The evanescent must, however,
be considered essential—not in the determination of something
fixed that is to be severed from the true and left lying outside it,
one does not know where; nor does the true rest on the other
side, dead and positive. The appearance is the coming to be and
passing away that does not come to be or pass away; it is in
itself and constitutes the actuality and the movement of the life
of the truth. The true is thus the bacchanalian whirl in which
no member is not drunken" (translated by Walter Kaufmann,
Hegel, p. 424).

[18] *Hegel's Science of Logic*, p. 735.

tence." [19] In mechanism, chemism, and teleology we find objectivity and determinateness; in teleology objectivity finally completes its escape from natural necessity into that free necessity which only self-determination can provide. As the truth of mechanism and chemism, end stands within the domain of objectivity where it is affected by externality and is confronted by an objective world to which it relates itself. "From this side," Hegel writes, "mechanical causality, which in general is to be taken as including chemism, still makes its appearance in this *end relation* which is the *external* one, but as *subordinate* to it and as sublated in and for itself." [20] Since mechanical and chemical objects are externally determined they lend themselves to being determined by the end relation.

Hegel's account of how the means-end relation of teleology utilizes the cause-effect relation of mechanism can now be examined. Hegel, as we have noted, was highly critical of pious, piecemeal applications of teleology which tend to explain happenings in the world in terms of external designs or ends, often of a most trivial sort. It was the inadequacy of such theories which led people to suppose, wrongly, that mechanism provides not only a more comprehensive but also a more immanent way of explaining what goes on in the world. In its high-

[19] *The Logic of Hegel,* p. 343.
[20] *Hegel's Science of Logic,* p. 740.

est form teleology, as depicted by Hegel, thinks of the world in terms of inner design and of an entirely immanent purposiveness. Hegel, however, does not begin his treatment of teleology by discussing teleology in its highest form. Instead he commences with a discussion of subjective end, which shares one characteristic with the pious, piecemeal versions of teleology which he has rejected: it involves a purposiveness which is imposed upon objects which are otherwise purposeless. In short, the subjective end uses but does not transform objects whose activities are explained, from the mechanical point of view, as being purposeless.

End, according to Hegel, is the subjective Concept as an essential effort and urge to posit itself externally. However, in this process it is exempt from transition: it is neither a force expressing itself nor a substance and cause manifesting itself in accidents and effects. Force has determinate being only in its expression; substance and cause have actuality only in their accidents and in their effects—their actuality in other words *is* transition. To be sure, Hegel concedes, end may also be spoken of as force or cause, but this can be done truthfully only if force and cause are predicated of end in a way which sublates their concept, as a force which solicits itself to expression or as a cause that is the cause of itself. End, Hegel continues, is the Concept that has reached itself in objectivity: "The determinateness it has given itself in that sphere is that of objective *indifference* to and *exter-*

nality of its determinedness." End as a determinate content is finite, although formally it is infinite subjectivity. Also, because its determinateness has the form of objective indifference, this determinateness has the shape of a presupposition: "From this side its finitude consists in its being confronted by an *objective*, mechanical and chemical *world* to which its actuality relates itself as to something *already* there." This world confronts the end "as a mechanical and chemical whole not yet determined and pervaded by end." [21]

The movement of end can be understood as aiming to sublate its presupposition, the immediacy of the object, and to posit the object as determined by the Concept. This aim is negative in its attitude toward the object, but it is also negative toward the end in its present condition, for it is the subjectivity of end which it seeks to sublate. Put positively, the movement of end has as its aim the realization of end, its union with objective being. Now the presupposition of objectivity shall be seen as posited by the Concept itself. What is posited by the Concept, however, is in the first instance not the realized end, the union of end with objective being; instead the object posited or determined by the Concept of end is so far only a *means:* "The end unites itself through a means with objectivity, and in objectivity with itself." [22]

Hegel speaks of the means as the middle term of a syllogism; as such it is external against both the extreme

[21] *Ibid.,* pp. 741–742. [22] *Ibid.,* p. 743.

of subjective end and the extreme of objective end. The means is only the mediating middle term because (*a*) it is an immediate object and (*b*) the relation it has to the extreme of end is an external one. Concept and objectivity are only externally combined in the means, "which is accordingly a merely *mechanical object.*" The means is an object *in itself* the totality of the Concept; it has no power of resistance against the end. In itself the means is identical with the end, but its lack of self-subsistence consists in the very fact that it is only *in itself* the totality of the Concept, for the Concept is a being-for-itself: "Consequently the object has the character of being powerless against the end and of serving it; the end is the object's subjectivity or soul, that has in the object its external side." The means has, however, a side from which it still enjoys some self-subsistence against the end: "The objectivity that is connected with the end in the means is still external to it, because it is only immediately so connected; and therefore, the presupposition still persists." [23] The end still has as its aim the overcoming of the presupposition of objectivity as something already there; this aim is not achieved so long as objectivity is posited in the means as something external. In this connection it is important to note that what had once been in the subjective end merely "an urge and a striving" is now an *activity*, as the end *acts* through the means in its attempt to realize itself.

[23] *Ibid.,* p. 745.

Following his treatment of the subjective end and of the means, Hegel undertakes an analysis of the realized end, with which he concludes his discussion of teleology. In its relation to the means the end, according to Hegel, is already reflected into itself, but its objective return into itself is not yet posited. If the activity of the end through its means were to consist again in merely determining the immediate objectivity, the product would be again merely a means, and so on *ad infinitum*. Always the product of the activity of the end would be only a means suitable to the end and not the objectivity of the end itself. To overcome this difficulty, the end, which is active in its means, must not in determining the immediate object act as a determinant external to the object; rather the object must spontaneously conform to the unity of the Concept: "The former external activity of the end through its means must determine itself as mediation and sublate its own self." [24] The mechanical and chemical processes emerge under the dominance of end, but the dominance satisfies the requirement specified by Hegel, namely that they spontaneously offer themselves to the end. Hegel argues that the negative attitude of end's purposive activity toward the object is not an external attitude but the transition of objectivity in its own self into the end.

Where the relation between end and object is concerned Hegel introduces a distinction between violence

[24] *Ibid.*, p. 746.

(*Gewalt*) and the "cunning of Reason." If the end relates itself immediately to an object and makes it a means
in determining another object, this is to be regarded as
violence insofar as the end appears to be of quite a
different nature from the object and the two objects (the
means and the object it will determine) are mutually
independent totalities. If, however, end posits itself in a
mediate relation with the object and interposes another
object between itself and the object it seeks to determine,
this may be thought of as the cunning of Reason. Earlier
in his treatment of the subjective end Hegel defined end
as "the *rational in its concrete existence*." The end, he
maintained, manifests rationality because it is the concrete Concept.[25] Hegel now proceeds to remind us of the
finitude of end and thus of the finitude of the rationality
of end when end enters into relationship with the object
conceived of as something external and already there,
not yet determined and pervaded by end. If end entered
into an immediate relation with the external object, end
would itself enter the domain of mechanism and chemism, with the result that it would be subject to contingency and the loss of its determinateness as the Concept
that is in and for itself. By putting forward an object as its means, however, the end avoids this surrender
to the world of contingency. The end allows the object
which it has put forward as a means "to wear itself out"
while the end "shields itself behind it from mechanical

[25] *Ibid.*, p. 741.

violence." In one important respect, however, the means thus employed is superior to the finite ends of external purposiveness. The plough, Hegel writes, is more honorable than the immediate enjoyment it procures: "In his tools man possesses power over external nature, even though in respect of his ends he is, on the contrary, subject to it." [26]

In treating the cunning of Reason Hegel notes, however, that it would be a mistake for us to think of the end as merely keeping outside the mechanical process: "rather it maintains itself in it and is its determination." As the Concept which freely exists in face of the object and its process and which is a self-determining activity, the end is also "the absolute truth" of mechanism and in mechanism the end is "only meeting with itself." The power of the end over the object is this "explicit identity"; the actuality of the end is the manifestation of it. The end as content is the determinateness that exists in and for itself, which appears in the object as indifferent and external, but the end as activity is at once both the truth of the process and what Hegel calls "the *sublating of the illusory show of externality*." [27]

Before clarifying what he means by 'the illusory show

[26] *Ibid.*, p. 747. Passages such as this falsify, I believe, two charges frequently levelled against Hegel, that he failed to appreciate man's dependence upon nature and that he was unaware of the importance of technology as a means of coping with this dependence.

[27] *Ibid.*, p. 747.

of externality' Hegel has some general and some specific remarks to make about the nature of the teleological process. The teleological process, Hegel writes, is the "translation" of the Concept which has a distinct concrete existence as a concept into objectivity; this translation is seen to be the meeting of the Concept with itself through itself. In all of its transitions the Concept remains itself. In the mechanical process when cause becomes effect it is only the cause meeting with itself in the effect.[28] By contrast in the teleological transition the Concept already has a concrete existence as cause (as the absolute concrete unity which is free from external determination), and the externality into which the end translates itself is itself already posited as a moment, or stage, of the Concept itself. Speaking most generally and with an air of surface paradox, Hegel says of the teleological activity that in it "the end is in the beginning, the consequent the ground, the effect the cause, that it is a becoming of what has become, that in it only what already exists comes into existence, and so forth." Hegel's explanation of why he speaks in this way is that "in general all the determinations of relationship belonging to the sphere of reflection of immediate being have lost their distinctions" and that what was once said to be an *other* is now posited as identical with the simple Con-

[28] Hegel believed, incorrectly, that the relation of cause and effect was "tautological." I discuss this question in Chapter Three.

cept.[29] Hegel's account of why he has strained language in this way can, however, be supplemented with the following remarks, which while incomplete might nevertheless help to explain the apparent paradox in what Hegel is saying. When Hegel writes that the end is in the beginning he is saying that the realized end is present in the subjective end as urge or inclination; when he writes that the consequent is the ground he is saying that objectivity is presupposed by the end; when he writes that the effect is the cause he is saying that when the Concept enters into a relationship with an object and uses that object as a means of realizing its own objectivity the effect of this use by the Concept of an object is a cause of the realization of the objectivity of the Concept; and when he writes of a becoming of what has become and of how that which already exists comes into existence, he is reminding us that as a distinct concept end already existed before it imposed itself upon the world of objects.

Hegel's more specific remarks about the teleological process show him to be still concerned with the problem of externality. Mechanical determinateness remains the paradigm case of externality, but a purposive activity which through its means has only a mechanical relation with its object is also defective in this regard. The product of such an external purposiveness can be, ac-

[29] *Ibid.*, p. 748.

cording to Hegel, only another means or a "relative end" and not a realized end: the determination here is "relative, external to the object itself and not objective." It is the "destiny" of whatever is intended to be used as a means toward the realization of an end that it be destroyed, Hegel writes, but he now attempts to show that the same destiny awaits the object that is supposed to contain the realized end and to represent the objectivity of the end. A house or a clock may appear as ends in relation to the tools used for their production, but the stones and beams or the wheels and axles which "constitute the actuality of the end" fulfill that end only through the physical and chemical pressures to which they are subjected. Thus they "fulfill their destiny only by being used and worn away . . . They are not positively united with the end, because they possess self-determination only externally and are only relative ends, or essentially nothing but means." Such ends have a limited *content*, although their *form* is the infinite self-determination of the Concept. They are ends inadequate to the infinity of the Concept, and they are "at the mercy of becoming and alteration and must pass away." [30]

Hegel's attempted solution to the problem of externality which he has posed is contained in his discussion of the realized end. The result of the teleological activity

[30] *Ibid.*, p. 750.

Hegel has been describing thus far is "not only an external end relation, but the truth of it, an internal end relation and an objective end." The externality of the object which the end presupposed is now described by Hegel as having been "an illusory show," and the activity of end is explained as being, "strictly speaking, only the representation of this illusory show and the sublating of it." In the realized end objectivity is present as the return of the end into itself; the means is taken up into the end and "vanishes." With it there also vanishes mediation itself as a relation of something external, and the end now has an immediate relation to its object. "The realized end," Hegel claims, "is also means, and conversely the truth of the means is just this, to be itself a real end." [31]

In the realized end there occurs the overt unity of subjective and objective: "the one-sided subjectivity and the show of objective independence confronting it are both cancelled." The realization of the implicit unity of subjective and objective is the Idea, which Hegel also defines as "truth in itself and for itself—the absolute unity of the notion [Concept] and objectivity." [32] The Idea, Hegel writes, may be described in many ways: as Reason; as subject-object; as the unity of the ideal and the real, of the finite and the infinite, of soul and body; as the possibility which has its actuality in its own self; and as that of which the nature can be thought only as

[31] *Ibid.*, pp. 751–752.   [32] *The Logic of Hegel*, pp. 351–352.

existent.[33] All these descriptions can be applied, according to Hegel, because the Idea contains all the relations of the Understanding, but contains them in their infinite self-return and self-identity.

If the externality of the object is illusory and if the object is implicitly the Concept all along, the illusion of externality nevertheless has its part to play in the scheme of things. Hegel writes that when the Concept in the shape of end is realized, we have but the manifestation of the inner nature of the object itself and thus objectivity (in the form of externality) is only a covering which conceals the Concept:

Within the range of the finite we can never see or experience that the End has been really secured. The consummation of the infinite End, therefore, consists merely in removing the illusion which makes it seem yet unaccomplished. The Good, the absolutely Good, is eternally accomplishing itself in the world: and the result is that it needs not wait upon us, but is already by implication, as well as in full actuality accomplished. This is the illusion under which we live. It alone supplies at the time the actualizing force on which the interest in the world reposes. In the course of its process the Idea creates that illusion, by

[33] *Ibid.*, p. 355. In the *Science of Logic*, p. 705, Hegel began his discussion of objectivity and of how the Concept determines itself into objectivity by remarking that it is "self-evident" that this transition is "identical" in character with what formerly appeared in metaphysics as the inference from the concept of God to his existence, or as the "so-called ontological proof of the existence of God."

setting an antithesis to confront it; and its action consists in getting rid of the illusion which it has created. Only out of this error does the truth arise. In this fact lies the reconciliation with error and with finitude. Error or other-being, when superseded, is still a necessary dynamic element of truth: for truth can only be where it makes itself its own result.[34]

The error or illusion of externality is thus necessary in several respects: it is a necessary condition of our interest and involvement in the world—if we knew that the Concept, in the shape of the end, was already present in the object, then we would have no further interest in seeing to it that the end was realized. Yet from the perspective of finite ends and within the limits of the Understanding we cannot know or experience the consummation of the infinite end, so the illusion is both a necessary condition of our activities and a necessary result of the limitations of our knowledge of the finite and our experiences thereof. Finally, the Idea needs the illusion of externality "as a necessary dynamic element of truth"— through overcoming this illusion the truth which is the Idea makes itself its own result.

Since Hegel's treatment of teleology provides the crucial transition in his system from the Concept to the Idea, and since this transition occurs at the point where the end becomes the realized end, it might be desirable to consider some of the difficulties which arise here be-

[34] *The Logic of Hegel*, pp. 351–352.

fore we return to our task of relating Hegel's reflections on teleology and mechanism to his philosophy of history. Some of these difficulties hinge, I believe, upon Hegel's account of how in the realized end the means vanishes into the end and the end is realized in the means. I propose to approach Hegel's account of the realized end in a somewhat gradual way and from the point of view of the means-end distinction as this is ordinarily understood. In this connection we need to provide several examples: first of something which is merely a means, second of something which is merely an end, third of an end which turns out to be in Hegel's words "a relative end" and thus a means, and fourth of an end which is realized in its means.

If we can conceive of a tool having no ornamental value or moral significance but being solely of instrumental value, this would do as an example of something which is merely a means. An example of something which is merely an end is perhaps even less difficult to provide—the secret ambition of a politician for a certain high office, an ambition which he never reveals to his associates and which is never achieved, will do here. Insofar as the tool does have some ornamental value or moral significance (here we may recall Hegel's point that man's tools may be more honorable than the pleasures he procures with them) and insofar as the ambition of the politician is revealed (perhaps he announces his candidacy but fails to win the office) our examples lose some of their purity, and what was merely a means or merely an end now becomes chiefly a means or chiefly a (subjective) end, but this wrinkle poses no problems for us here. Hegel has already provided us in his examples of the clock and the house with illustrations of subjective ends which although they are realized turn out to be "relative" ends and thus means. Perhaps significantly, Hegel gives no examples of an end which is realized in its means, and in casting about for illustrations of such an end one might be tempted to reconsider the clock and house examples. It is, however, difficult to see how the examples of the clock and the house could be reinterpreted so as to save them from the limitations Hegel has already noted or implied. The relationship of a house to the end of providing shelter is after all "external" or contingent in several important respects: the house may fall or burn down, the house is only one of many houses, and only one of several ways a man might find shelter, and so on.

A possible example of an end which is realized in its means might be the following: a man writes a book in order to earn money in order to have the leisure in which to write more books. One might say that this man is writing in order to write and that here the end is realized in the means and the means vanishes in the end. But even with this example certain objections might be raised: writing a book in this case is a means to writing *other* books, or writing the book in question is a means of securing money which is a means of securing leisure which is a means of enabling the author to go on writing. Here the difficulty of externality or contingency which was so harmful to the house and clock examples reappears: the money may prove insufficient; if it is sufficient, the author's leisure may be disturbed by war or ill health; or his abilities may simply prove unequal to the task he has set himself. Even if the example could survive in the face of these objections, it would still be extremely difficult to picture the entire world of objects and ends as fitting the model suggested by this example, but then I doubt whether any single example could suggest an adequate model for all that Hegel has in mind when he seeks to overcome the illusion of externality.

In seeking to overcome the illusion of externality Hegel is not denying what philosophers call "the existence of the external world." Rather he is insisting upon the immanent purposiveness of that external world which, he maintains, exists in order to call forth the self-consciousness of the Spirit. In this connection our example of the writer who writes in order to write has some value, provided we flesh out the story along the following lines: nature provides raw materials out of which men manufacture pens and typewriters; these artifacts, however, are not the end but rather the objects of the manufacturing process; they and the materials from which they are made are in time broken or worn out (Hegel would say rather grandly "they fulfill their destiny") by being used for ends such as the writing of a book; without them, however, the idea of writing a book might not have occurred to the author or, having occurred, might have remained a subjective fancy of his; finally, the writing of a book becomes a means to the end of writing other books but here the end is realized, at least in part, in its means—put somewhat differently, the end of the activity is the activity itself. The project of writing other books might be seen as undertaking a vocation which has as its end an ever-growing self-awareness, and this vocation is but an extension or continuation of that act of (systematic) self-awareness which constitutes the author's initial work.

Whether one believes that Hegel has dispelled the illusion of externality depends upon whether one accepts the perspective of immanent purposiveness from which the separation of objects and ends is finally seen as illusory. Our example of the author who writes in order to write does not become fully Hegelian until one interprets it as illustrating the thesis that nature, technology, and Spirit all exist *in order to* promote acts of self-awareness on the part of the Spirit. It would plainly not be enough to satisfy Hegel if we were only able to show that acts of self-awareness such as writing are in point of fact the products of the interaction of nature, technology, and Spirit—this would be to confuse *products, results,* or *effects* with *ends.* Moreover, to keep Hegel's teleology safe from that triviality apparent in statements like 'Nature, technology, and Spirit exist so that Jones may write his book'—a triviality of which Hegel was a severe critic—the purposiveness in question must be shown to be both immanent in the world and identified with an *infinite* end, the self-awareness of Spirit in all its forms, and not restricted to any single finite end. One additional if obvious point needs making about the writing example: Hegel is not interested in this connection in whether it might be inspirational to believe that nature, technology, and Spirit are purposively engaged in furthering acts of self-awareness on the part of Spirit, but in whether it is true that nature, technology, and Spirit are so engaged.

Hegel, of course, maintained that it is true and that he had shown it to be true. Most of his readers today are doubtful, and I am no more inclined to campaign for the resurrection of Hegel's immanent teleology than Walter Kaufmann or J. N. Findlay is to labor for the resurrection of Hegel's dialectic. Appreciation does not entail acceptance, but the failure to accept a position or perspective does not prevent us from appreciating the significance of the position or perspective in question or from making various uses of it.[35] At the minimum it is

[35] Hegel appears to have believed that the history of philosophy is necessarily evaluative. Speaking of W. G. Tennemann's *Geschichte der Philosophie*, he writes "Tennemann thinks that it is really the case that the historian should have no philosophy, and he glories in that; yet he really has a system and he is a critical philosopher. He praises philosophers, their work and

still open to us to attempt to use one position taken by an author as a key to unlock or explain other positions he holds, and Hegel's teleological doctrine seems the most likely key for unlocking his views about the relation of philosophical history to other varieties of history and ultimately for understanding his conception of the historical process itself.

Teleology, Mechanism, and the Study of Human History

Hegel's discussion of how mechanism and chemism are sublated in teleology recalls Hegel's treatment of the relations between original and reflective history and philosophical history. To be sure, Hegel does not say that original and reflective history are *sublated* in philosophical history, but there seems to be no good reason why, apart from a regard for the sensitivity of the practicing historian, he could not have used this word with its curious, dual flavor of preservation *and* going beyond. The parallels between the two aspects of Hegel's thought

---

their genius, and yet the end of the lay is that all of them will be pronounced to be wanting in that they have one defect, which is not to be Kantian philosophers." Hegel also writes that "In external history everything is in action—certainly there is in it what is important and that which is unimportant—but action is the idea immediately placed before us. This is not the case in Philosophy, and on this account the history of Philosophy cannot be treated throughout without the introduction of the historian's views" (*Lectures on the History of Philosophy*, I,

are numerous and important, which is scarcely surprising given that Hegel's teleological approach to the study of history is best regarded as an instance of his teleological approach to the world in general. In the light of Hegel's theoretical analysis of teleology, especially in the *Science of Logic*, it becomes clearer why it is that the teleological question about the ultimate purpose of the world is not just the last question that Hegel happened to ask about history but the ultimate question which determines the value and significance—but not the content—of answers to all other questions about history. Once we have noted the parallels between Hegel's analysis of teleology and mechanism and Hegel's dissection of the varieties of historical inquiry the problem arises, however, as to whether there is an exact parallel in one crucial respect. The problem concerns whether original history and reflective history, or perhaps only one of these, stand in the same relation to mechanism as philosophical history stands in relation to teleology. While its solution may be on a certain

---

pp. 113-114, p. 116). See also W. H. Walsh's "Hegel on the History of Philosophy," *History and Theory* (1965), *Beiheft* V, pp. 67-82. Walsh argues, in partial support of Hegel's conception of the history of philosophy, that many such histories even when written by non-Hegelians do involve assessments of past philosophical positions. I have no quarrel with this claim, but I do believe Hegel's claim that the history of philosophy is necessarily evaluative to be mistaken. Reconstruction and assessment while they may occur together are nevertheless distinct activities.

level fairly obvious, this problem nevertheless calls our attention to some interesting difficulties in that area where Hegel's philosophy of history and his philosophy of science rub shoulders; it also opens up once more and from a somewhat different perspective the question of how important Hegel's distinctions among the varieties of historical inquiry really are.

Where the latter question is concerned there are two inclinations among commentators: one is to minimize the importance of the distinctions Hegel makes among the varieties of historical inquiry, while the other is to exaggerate their importance. Of these two inclinations the second is the more harmful, but both inclinations stem from an incorrect appraisal of what Hegel was attempting to do. To minimize the importance of Hegel's distinctions two steps may be taken: the difference between reflective history and philosophical history, both being in a sense contemplative activities, can be represented as imprecise; next the difference between original history, which is modeled on reports of perception, and other kinds of history can be minimized since perception is considered by Hegel to be "more or less a species" of reflection. The suggestion can then be advanced that "Hegel used his classification of kinds of histories merely as a rhetorical device, as a way of establishing an initial rapport with a nonphilosophical audience." [36] To deny

[36] Haskell Fain, *Between Philosophy and History* (Princeton, 1970), pp. 69–70.

that Hegel's distinctions among the varieties of historical
inquiry are hard and inviolate is to some extent in the
spirit of Hegel himself who repeatedly warned against
making too much of any distinction. However, perception might, as Hegel thought, necessarily have a cognitive
element without thereby becoming reflection; and reflective history may not be reflective in the same way that
philosophical history is reflective; finally, to speak of
Hegel's distinctions or classifications as "a rhetorical
device" aimed at "a nonphilosophical audience" falls
short of the truth on two counts: there is no reason to
suppose that the audience which heard Hegel's lectures—
or the eventual audience he may have had in mind—was
nonphilosophical; also even if Hegel's audience had been
nonphilosophical the "rhetorical device" interpretation
of Hegel's distinctions downgrades a serious philosophical exploration of, among other things, the relation of
the empirical and the a priori in historical investigation
into a mere literary gambit.

The second inclination, while more harmful, is also the
more interesting. Here the impulse is to drive a sharp
wedge between original and reflective history and philosophical history, to consider original and reflective history empirical and philosophical history a priori, to
regard empirical history as being in large measure concerned with explanations in terms of efficient causes and
with tracing the workings of general laws in history
and to regard a priori history as being an attempt "to get
beyond the empirical standpoint altogether and approach

it in quite another way" and to deduce the outlines of the historical process from "purely philosophical premises." [37] I take this to be the essence of W. H. Walsh's interpretation of Hegel. For us such an interpretation poses three basic questions: (1) whether getting beyond the empirical standpoint means for Hegel getting altogether beyond this standpoint; (2) whether Walsh has characterized the empirical standpoint of the historian in a manner which would approximate what Hegel has in mind when he speaks of this standpoint or orientation; and (3) what Walsh thinks Hegel's a priori approach to history involves. The answer to (1) depends upon the answer to (2). If Walsh has correctly characterized the empirical standpoint of the historian as involving a concern with efficient causes and general laws, then it seems fair to say that Hegel did perhaps want to get altogether beyond this standpoint. However, for reasons which I

[37] W. H. Walsh, *An Introduction to the Philosophy of History* (London, 1953), pp. 149–151. Walsh also writes, p. 150, "the suggestion that we explain an historical event when we sort out the different causal factors at work in it and estimate their importance would not content him: he wanted more explanation than that. And by 'more' in this connection he did not mean more explanation of the same kind as before. It was not the incompleteness of the story told by working historians which distressed him; it was its essential superficiality." In my judgment it was the incompleteness of the story told by working historians which mainly concerned Hegel; at any rate, while Hegel did regard certain individual historians as superficial, only one variety of ordinary history, the pragmatic, seemed to Hegel superficial, and even pragmatic history did not seem to him always or necessarily superficial.

shall try to make clearly shortly, Hegel would deny that Walsh has correctly characterized the empirical standpoint of the historian and would most likely insist that Walsh has succeeded only in characterizing the empirical standpoint of the natural scientist. Thus, I believe Hegel's professed respect for the empirical standpoint of the historian should override the claim that Hegel wanted to get altogether beyond this standpoint, especially when this standpoint is analyzed in terms which would be unacceptable to Hegel. (Of course, Hegel wanted to get beyond the empirical standpoint of the historian in some respects else he would not have bothered being a philosopher of history, but that is not being contested here.)

Where (3) is concerned Walsh seems to have in mind only the familiar charge that Hegel sought to deduce the outlines of the historical process from "purely philosophical premises" (which is, of course, an improvement upon the older charge that Hegel sought to deduce both the outlines and the details of the historical process in this manner). However, Walsh in setting forth this argument makes the following interesting observation: "Hegel asks the question 'why?' about history in a sense different from that in which it is asked by working historians; or rather . . . he asks 'why?' first in the straightforward historical sense or senses, and then in a further sense of his own." [38] Walsh does not specify what this further sense is, but if my interpretation of Hegel's conception

[38] *Ibid.*, p. 150.

of philosophical history is correct this further sense can only be the teleological sense. With this supplement to Walsh's position, I wish now to go further than Walsh does by extending the argument under consideration along the following lines. Let us suppose for the moment that Walsh's analysis of the empirical standpoint of the historian is correct after all, that the historian does ask his 'why' question in pursuit of efficient causes and general laws, and let us also suppose that the philosopher of history asks his 'why' question in a quest for final causes or ultimate purposes. Now, recalling that mechanism characteristically employs the language of cause-effect and teleology the language of ultimate purpose and of the means-end relation, can we say that original history and reflective history are species of mechanism and philosophical history is a species of teleology? And if not, can we show that such an interpretation attaches the wrong kind of importance to Hegel's distinction between philosophical history and the other varieties of history by plugging in Hegel's distinction between mechanism and teleology at the wrong place?

The basic reason why original history and reflective history should not be interpreted as being species of mechanism lies in their subject matter, the past actions of men in which, according to Hegel, Spirit, not nature, is the distinguishing mark. If Hegel is correct, the successes of mechanism are largely in the domain of the prespiritual and the extrahistorical. If my interpretation of

Hegel is correct, he is not saying that mechanism is false as an account of certain aspects of human behavior but rather that it is insufficient or incomplete because of its failure to capture the distinctively human. Some support for Hegel's downgrading of mechanism in this way may be found in the fact that practicing historians rarely if ever mention mechanical or physical laws in their accounts of historical phenomena. An Hegelian interpretation of this fact might proceed as follows: historians by omitting to mention physical, chemical, or biological laws in no way mean to convey the impression that they do not believe such laws to be among the necessary and sufficient conditions for the occurrence of various historical phenomena. But while historians take the presence of such laws for granted, their failure to mention them in their explanations of historical phenomena is a sign of something other than casualness or haste. It reflects rather the historian's sound intuition that historical writing is not the proper place to make mention of physical, chemical, or biological laws, for the practicing historian (whatever his professed philosophical sympathies may be) does not in the final analysis actually believe that significant human actions are simply a function of physical, chemical, or biological forces. A physical condition may cause a man to sneeze but that is hardly if ever a significant human action, if it is an action at all; and it is significant, and distinctively human, action with which the historian is concerned. The underlying metaphysic of the practicing historian, as articulated by the Hegelian, is that the historian concerns himself with a subject matter which may be said, quite sensibly and without fear of self-contradiction, to be a cause of itself. (In *The Philosophy of Right*, p. 53, Hegel applies to Spirit Spinoza's definition of substance as a cause of itself.) And this is a subject matter common to original, reflective, and philosophical histories alike, whatever their differences might be.

While mechanism is informative mainly about the background against which human actions take place, several complexities in Hegel's treatment of mechanism need noting and this will involve a brief recapitulation of several things said earlier. First, while Hegel emphatically refuses to accept mechanism as an "absolute category" and indeed regards it as "a shallow and superficial mode of inquiry" he nevertheless recognizes that mechanism (the first form of objectivity) has "the right and import of a general logical category" [39] with applications even to the world of the mind. In a more modern language one could say that here Hegel seems to be denying that the application of the category of mechanism to mental activities and human actions necessarily involves a "category mistake" and is in fact claiming that there are instances of the successful application of mechanism in these areas. This brings us to our second problem: what significance are we to attach to the phenomena noted by

[39] *The Logic of Hegel*, p. 338.

Hegel as instances of the success of mechanism in this regard? We are right, according to Hegel, in speaking of a mechanical memory, and we may also be correct in speaking of an act of reading or of writing or the playing of a musical instrument as being mechanical. In fact, however, as Hegel also notes, our use of mechanical idioms in describing mental activities and human actions isn't very common; carrying Hegel's argument one step further, one could note that when such a way of speaking is employed it is often a way of indicating that something has gone wrong—some failure on the part of the agent is being noted. Or else such cases might be explained, by someone in sympathy with the Hegelian point of view, in terms of habit (which Hegel defined as a tensionless activity from which the struggle, the difficulty, and hence much of the point has disappeared) or as marking a rather low level activity in which mind or Spirit was scarcely involved to begin with.

The third complexity in Hegel's treatment of mechanism to which I wish to call attention is also the most troublesome, for it concerns cases not in which the mind or Spirit is merely absent in varying degrees from its own activities but cases in which Spirit is estranged from itself. When self-consciousness opposes itself to its objective universality and estranges itself from it, by this separation the subject is converted into an object and is brought into the relationship of externality to its own essence or nature, which means that it can now be treated under the category of mechanism.[40] In this relationship of externality the object is no longer to be considered the cause of itself but as being causally determined by forces outside itself. And yet some degree of estrangement is necessary for the development of self-consciousness or the realization of the Spirit: a nation or a person without deeds is without blame but such a nation or person also lacks actuality. Action for Hegel *necessarily* involves some measure of self-estrangement, of turning away from one's objective universality. And in the turning away, doesn't one become necessarily involved in mechanical relationships in which one's behavior is accountable for in the language of cause-effect rather than that of means-end, even though ultimately if the process of self-realization is complete these causal accounts are sublated in teleological ones? However, in another section of the *Science of Logic* Hegel argues that the application of the category of causality to spiritual life and even to physico-organic life is inadmissible. He writes that "it is inadmissible to say that food is the *cause* of blood, or certain dishes or chill and damp are the *causes* of fever, and so on; it is equally inadmissible to assign the ionic climate as the *cause* of Homer's works, or Caesar's ambition as the *cause* of the downfall of the republican constitution of Rome. In history generally, spiritual masses and individuals are in play and reciprocal-determination with one another; but it is rather the nature of

[40] See pages 720–721 of *Hegel's Science of Logic*.

spirit, in a much higher sense than it is the character of the living thing in general, not to receive into itself another *original* entity, or not to let a cause continue itself into it but to break it off and to transmute it." [41]

The difficulty here is that on the one hand Hegel conceives of Spirit as being estranged from itself and thus entering the domain of mechanism as part of its journey toward complete self-realization while on the other hand he denies that Spirit is to be dealt with in the language of efficient causality which is, of course, the language of mechanism. This problem is further accentuated by Hegel's belief that estrangement is necessary to Spirit's development. In the *Phenomenology* Hegel writes that Spirit necessarily appears in time and that time is "spirit's destiny and necessity, where spirit is not yet complete within itself"; [42] being incomplete and thus in time Spirit necessarily undergoes some degree of estrangement. I think, however, that this difficulty in Hegel need not involve a contradiction. While Spirit is not complete and is thus involved in time, in history, the mark which Hegel believes distinguishes historical man from pre-historical man is that historical man knows who he is and what he wants. This knowledge may be at the beginning of history quite rudimentary, and the main text of Hegel's *Philosophy of History* is devoted to

[41] *Ibid.*, p. 562. See also *The Logic of Hegel*, p. 281.

[42] *The Phenomenology of Mind*, translated by J. B. Baillie (London, 1961), p. 800.

tracing historically an ever-increasing but not yet complete sophistication in man's self-awareness or self-consciousness. But to the extent that historical man does know who he is and what he wants he does not receive into himself another original entity but breaks it off and transmutes it. These metaphors of Hegel's seem clear enough to convey the basic point which I believe Hegel wishes to make: that an ever-increasing self-consciousness in man involves an ever-decreasing applicability of the category of causality and the mechanical point of view to his actions. As man becomes more self-conscious the category of causality and the mechanical point of view become more and more restricted to an explanation of what Hegel speaks of as "the background" or "the occasion" or "the external stimulus" of man's actions. (Perhaps it should be noted here, in view of the debate current in our time over the problem of historical explanation, that while on Hegel's view man as he grows in self-consciousness will undoubtedly perform increasingly complex actions, it is not the complexity *per se* of human actions that makes them increasingly less suitable for causal-mechanical analysis. Also, while Hegel would presumably want to say that each particular human action is in some nontrivial sense unique, he does not explicitly invoke this argument as a means of pointing out the limits of causal-mechanical analyses of human action.)

The relevance of the above discussion to Hegel's distinctions among the varieties of history is, I suggest, chiefly the following: estrangement and the problems it brings with it cannot mark the differences between original, reflective, and philosophical history. So long as man is condemned to an historical existence, history will have this estrangement and the attendant conversion of the subject into an object as part of its data, regardless of whether the scope of its inquiry is narrow (original history) or wide (reflective history) or comprehensive (philosophical history). To be sure, there will be in this connection a difference separating original and reflective history from philosophical history, but this difference will not be the difference between mechanical and teleological modes of inquiry. Rather it will consist in the following: original and reflective history, being necessarily limited to that part of man's history which is already past, can record the extent to which man has progressed beyond the domain of mechanism into the domain of teleology where self-consciousness and freedom predominate; philosophical history with its knowledge of the ultimate purpose immanent in the world can provide criteria for distinguishing what is essential and necessary in man's past actions from what is accidental and contingent, and philosophical history can describe the general features of a human existence in which mechanism is sublated in teleology. In this respect it would be correct to say, but in a sense quite different from that intended by Walsh, that Hegel's philosophical history does seek to provide an outline of the historical process if by this we mean not an outline of what man will actually do but an outline of what man can do. Hegel's philosophical history attempts to provide such an outline by a twofold process. If as Hegel believes a man is what he does and if this is true of mankind as a whole, then the history of man's development thus far provides a significant clue as to what man can do; this helps explain Hegel's insistence that the philosopher take seriously the empirical data supplied by the professional historian. It is also true, according to Hegel, that the philosopher by a logical (we would say metaphysical) analysis of the Idea and the ultimate purpose of the world can also determine what it is that man can accomplish by way of self-realization. But whether one is doing original and reflective history or philosophical history one's mode of inquiry is essentially teleological, reflecting the purposive nature of the subject matter, man.

This purposive nature of man has two aspects: first, there are individual agents consciously pursuing certain specific ends or goals which they hope to realize; second, there are the ends or goals of freedom and self-consciousness which belong to man *qua* man and which, Hegel believes, are usually but not always furthered by the interaction of individual agents in pursuit of their particular ends or goals and which are furthered independently of whether *any* of the individual agents in question consciously pursue them. Under both aspects of man's purposive nature the relationship of teleology to mechanism is essentially the same: cause-effect relationships are sublated or taken up into means-end relationships.

Where the relationship of the two aspects or dimensions of man's purposive nature is concerned, Herbert Marcuse holds a view which differs significantly from the one I have outlined above. Because his view has been widely influential and because a discussion of his interpretation of Hegel leads naturally into the next topic I wish to consider, namely the relationship of necessity and contingency in Hegel's philosophy of history, I hope that what is in effect a fairly long parenthesis will be permissible at this point. While rightly recognizing that for Hegel any "laws" which explain human history will differ in kind from scientific laws such as those which govern matter, Marcuse argues that the law or laws governing human history ultimately depend upon man's recognition of them and his determination to execute them. Thus man's freedom and the self-consciousness of freedom appear to depend, on Marcuse's interpretation of Hegel, upon at least some individual agents having freedom and the self-consciousness of freedom as ends or goals which they consciously pursue: "The universal law of history is, in Hegel's formulation, not simply progress to freedom, but progress 'in the self-consciousness of freedom.' A set of historical tendencies becomes a law only if man comprehends and acts on them. Historical laws, in other words, originate and are actual only in man's conscious practice, so that *if, for instance, there is a law of progress to ever higher forms of freedom, it ceases to operate if man fails to recognize and execute it.* Hegel's philosophy of history might amount to a deterministic theory, but the determining factor is at least freedom. *Progress depends on man's ability to grasp the universal interest of reason and on his will and vigor in making it a reality.*" [43]

This passage poses numerous difficulties: (1) What kind of "law" is it that depends for its validity upon man's comprehending and acting upon it? When belief and acting upon a belief enter the picture in this way aren't we more inclined to speak of a "self-fulfilling prophecy" than a "law"? (2) How can historical "tendencies" or trends "become" a law? Popper accuses Hegel of confusing laws with tendencies or trends, but this accusation seems to fit Marcuse better than Hegel. However, since Popper in a neglected footnote allows that if we are successful in determining "the complete or sufficient conditions c of a singular trend t, then we can formulate the universal law: 'Whenever there are conditions of the kind c there will be a trend of the kind t'," [44] this confusion can be regarded as a mere confusion and not as necessarily fatal to Marcuse's (or Hegel's) argument. What would be fatal, if Popper is correct as I believe he is, would be the confusion of laws with "abso-

[43] *Reason and Revolution, Hegel and the Rise of Social Theory* (Boston, 1954), p. 231. My italics.
[44] *The Poverty of Historicism* (New York, 1961), p. 129, n. 1.

lute trends" (trends which are mistakenly believed to be unconditional and irreversible). (3) Most seriously of all, Marcuse's interpretation of Hegel ignores the central point of Hegel's remarks concerning the cunning of Reason, which Hegel sees as going *against* man's will and conscious intentions to achieve its ends or goals for man. Whatever reservations one may have about exactly how informative this metaphor of Hegel's is, its principal thrust is to underscore the claim that man's freedom and self-consciousness may be attained regardless of whether any individual agents consciously pursue these ends, either for themselves as individuals or for mankind in general. If I may use Popperian language to make an Hegelian point, Hegel in speaking of the cunning of Reason acknowledges the importance of the unintended consequences of intentional human actions and then argues, in a markedly non-Popperian way, that most but not all of these consequences can be viewed teleologically as furthering man's freedom and the self-consciousness of freedom. Of course, once man is free and self-conscious then he will be aware of his freedom, as the "law" of his nature, but this is not at issue here. (4) If, as Marcuse maintains, Hegel thought that progress depends upon "man's ability to grasp the universal interest of reason and on his will and vigor in making it a reality," is it fair to ask which men Hegel believed have such ability, will and vigor? Philosophers (after reading Hegel) might have the ability to grasp the universal interest of reason, but Hegel denies them an active role in the historical process and condemns them to an essentially retrospective analysis of shapes of life; world historical individuals or heroes have the will and vigor to advance the universal interest of reason but Hegel's treatment of the extent to which they comprehend the universal interest of reason is ambivalent. On the one hand he speaks of them as seers who grasp a higher universal and make it their purpose, but on the other hand he insists that they are practical, political men who have no consciousness of the Idea as such.[45] All we can be sure of is that they possess insight into "what is needed and timely," but the gap which may exist between what someone like Caesar may take, perhaps correctly, to be "needed and timely" and a consciousness of and commitment to ever higher forms of freedom is obvious.[46] The cunning of Reason,

[45] *Reason in History*, pp. 39–40. See Shlomo Avineri, "Consciousness and History: *List der Vernunft* in Hegel and Marx," in *New Studies in Hegel's Philosophy*, edited by W. E. Steinkraus (New York, 1971), p. 112: "Those who act in history do not understand it, and those who understand it do not act upon it. . . . it always remains an open problem whether anyone except the philosopher shares the consciousness of progressing toward the consciousness of freedom."

[46] Some critics are persuaded that either intentionally or in effect Hegel blurs the distinction between "what is needed and timely" and what is philosophically justifiable, and certainly Hegel did insist that philosophers not ignore the needs of the times in their evaluation of institutions and actions. However, Hegel at times also makes a sharp distinction between historical justification and philosophical justification. The appeal to cir-

and not the rationality of any particular kind(s) of historical agents, is, I think, Hegel's attempt to bridge this critical gap.

Marcuse has nevertheless come upon an important point in Hegel's philosophy, namely that man's freedom and the self-consciousness of freedom may not as a matter of fact ever be fully actualized. Hegel in his *Lectures on the Philosophy of Religion* writes that *"in human*

cumstances, to the needs of the times, may he believed turn out to be in some cases the opposite of a more general or philosophical justification: if the justification of an institution or an action is made out solely in terms of its satisfying circumstances that obtain at a given time, then when these circumstances cease to exist so, too, does the justification which depends upon them. "By dint of obscuring the difference between the historical and the philosophical study of law, it becomes possible to shift the point of view and slip over from the problem of the true justification of a thing to a justification by appeal to circumstances, to deductions from presupposed conditions which in themselves may have no higher validity, and so forth. To generalize, by this means the relative is put in place of the absolute and the external appearance in place of the true nature of the thing. When those who try to justify things on historical grounds confound an origin in external circumstances with one in the concept, they unconsciously achieve the very opposite of what they intend. Once the origination of an institution has been shown to be wholly to the purpose and necessary in the circumstances of the time, the demands of history have been fulfilled. But if this is supposed to pass for a general justification of the thing itself, it turns out to be the opposite, because since those circumstances are no longer present, the institution so far from being justified has by their disappearance lost its meaning and its right. Suppose, for example, that we accept

freedom what is and what ought to be are separate. This freedom brings with it the power of free choice, and it is possible for it to sever itself from its necessity, from its laws, and to work in opposition to its true destiny." [47] This point can, however, be made independently of how one decides the question of whether man in order to realize his destiny must consciously embrace freedom and the self-consciousness of freedom as his goals or ends. Moreover, it is questionable whether Marcuse fully appreciates the possibility that man in Hegel's view may not actualize all his potentials for freedom and self-consciousness: to do this one would have to allow contingency or the possibility of failure a greater part in Hegel's philosophy than Marcuse seems willing to recognize. To be sure, Marcuse writes that "Necessity presupposes a reality that is contingent, that is, one which in its prevailing form holds possibilities that are not realized" [48] but the crucial question is whether there are possibilities that may *never* be realized—this is what gen-

---

as a vindication of the monasteries their service in cultivating wildernesses and populating them, in keeping learning alive by transcribing manuscripts and giving instruction, &c., and suppose further that this service has been deemed to be the ground and the purpose of their continued existence, then what really follows from considering this past service is that, since circumstances have now entirely altered, the monasteries are at least in this respect superfluous and inappropriate" (*The Philosophy of Right*, pp. 17–18).

[47] *Op. cit.*, I, p. 5. My italics.   [48] Marcuse, *op. cit.*, p. 153.

uine contingency would require. Here Marcuse seems inclined to give necessity the upper hand, although his choice of language leaves room for some doubt: "Regress, when it occurs, is not an 'external contingency' but, as we shall see, is part of the dialectic of historical change. . . . Every obstacle on the road to freedom is surmountable, given the efforts of a self-conscious mankind." [49] But the question is whether mankind's efforts will necessarily suffice? In his Preface Marcuse writes: "It *may even be* justifiable, logically as well as historically, to define Reason in terms which include slavery, the Inquisition, child labor, concentration camps, gas chambers, and nuclear preparedness. These *may well have been* integral parts of that rationality which has governed the recorded history of mankind." [50] To which one might reply: of course, things may turn out this way, but then they may not. It all depends on whether genuine contingency has any part to play here, or whether we can be sure in advance that contingency will always—necessarily?—be putty in the hands of a necessity which will not rest until all man's potentials for freedom and self-consciousness have been fully actualized.

[49] *Ibid.*, p. 231.   [50] *Ibid.*, p. xii. My italics.

CHAPTER THREE

Contingency and Necessity

Iris Murdoch has written, most perceptively, "It is always a significant question to ask about any philosopher: what is he afraid of?" [1] If this question were asked of Hegel, the answer would be that he is most afraid of contingency. It could be argued that for Hegel contingency, or as he sometimes says accident or chance, is our most effective *memento mori* and thus the most significant obstacle in the search for necessity and meaning in the life of historical man. In this connection we need only to recall that famous passage in which Hegel speaks of history as "the slaughter-bench at which the happiness of peoples, the wisdom of states, and the virtues of individuals have been sacrificed" and his concern over the "moral sadness," the "boredom," and the retreat into selfishness which this way of looking at history could easily produce in us. [2]

[1] *The Sovereignty of Good* (New York, 1971), p. 72.
[2] *Reason in History*, pp. 26–27.

How Contingency Is "Sublated" in Necessity

It has frequently been argued that Hegel's fear of contingency was so great that he sought either to explain it away as mere appearance or to explain it in terms of its contribution to some higher necessity. Characterizing teleologists in general, Isaiah Berlin has written, "For the teleological thinker all apparent disorder, inexplicable disaster, gratuitous suffering, unintelligible concatenations of random events are due not to the nature of things but to our failure to discover their purpose." [3] While this is an apt generalization which fits many teleologists, it does not, I shall argue, apply to Hegel: on my interpretation, Hegel believed that some "apparent disorders," some "inexplicable disasters," *et cetera* will remain very much with us, resisting the efforts of the philosopher or the philosophical historian either to explain them away as mere appearance or to explain them as means toward the realization of some higher goal, end, or purpose. For example, we might have to conclude that the disorders caused by Hitler were not apparent but all too real and also that we can not discover their "purpose." Our "failure to discover their purpose" may be due not to any real failure on our part but rather to the nature of things, or in other words the "failure" of the most subtle dialectical reasoning to discern how this disorder has contributed to the growth of human free-

[3] *Historical Inevitability*, p. 17.

dom may be due to the fact that no contribution was made, that here the results were entirely and forever negative. Hegel, I believe, wished to say: (1) that we use the categories of contingency and necessity in interpreting the world around us, (2) that there actually are instances of both categories in the world around us, and (3) that not every instance of contingency in the world around us can be explained in terms of its contribution to some higher necessity. Of the species man, for example, Hegel would want to say that it is necessarily rational and yet resist saying of every particular man either that he is rational or that his actions even when irrational or nonrational must in every case serve some higher (rational) purpose or end.

It is easy enough to find passages in which Hegel appears to favor necessity at the expense of contingency. Early in the *Lectures on the History of Philosophy* Hegel defines philosophy as "the science of necessity" and later he observes that "Contingency must vanish on the appearance of Philosophy." [4] To be sure, Hegel in

[4] *Op. cit.*, I, pp. 12, 36–37. It was in this connection that Hegel argued that "every philosophy has been and still is necessary" and that "no philosophy has ever been refuted. What has been refuted is not the principle of this philosophy, but merely the fact that this principle should be considered final and absolute in character" (p. 37). Hegel's claims have, of course, been the occasion of much controversy centering chiefly upon (*a*) whether Hegel regarded his own philosophy as final and absolute and thus exempt from the history that had befallen all preceding philosophies and (*b*) what sense should be attached

these passages is discussing the role of contingency in the history of philosophy, and philosophy is special in the sense of being an especially rational discipline in which, if Hegel is correct, one has good reasons to expect the role of contingency to be minimal; nevertheless, extrapolation from this special context to the world in general has seemed to many commentators eminently justifiable. On the other hand, though admittedly with greater difficulty, one can also find in Hegel passages in which contingency does not seem about to vanish, on the appearance of philosophy or anything else. In the *Phenomenology* Hegel in analyzing the relationship of the unchanging consciousness to the particular consciousness writes, "For the latter it is thus altogether a contingency, a mere chance event, that the unchangeable receives the form of particularity." Hegel goes on

---

to his statement that no philosophy has ever been refuted. Stated somewhat differently, the problem posed by (*a*) and (*b*) is this: isn't the claim that no philosophy is ever refuted itself refuted if it can be shown that, as Hegel believed, all or most philosophical "principles" are not "final and absolute in character"? Significantly Hegel himself observes a few sentences later in the above passage that "The atomic theory has been refuted, and we are atomists no longer." By this Hegel means, I think, that the atom is no longer conceived of as "the absolute existence" or the ultimate unit of study; but if this is so, then what could count as the principle of the atomic theory (or philosophical atomism) that has remained unrefuted? Presumably, that there *are* atoms or atomic units and that these constitute if not ultimate then nevertheless important and intelligible units of study.

to speak of this union of the unchangeable and the particular as being also due in part to the nature of the unchangeable, thus suggesting that the particular consciousness may have overstated the importance of contingency in this matter. Later, however, he speaks of the gap between the hope of a union of the individual consciousness with the unchangeable consciousness and the fruition of this union in these terms: "between the hope and fulfillment there stands precisely the absolute contingency or immovable indifference, which is involved in the very assumption of determinate shape and form, the basis and foundation of the hope." [5] Thus it appears that contingency while it is to be explained is not to be explained away, is not to be relegated to the realm of mere appearance. Contingency of the sort depicted here will not "vanish" when its relations to necessity have been explained; and I shall also try to show that not all contingency (not every instance of contingency) will lend itself to philosophical analysis in terms of its relation to necessity, and that instances of hard-core or brute contingency need not, and on Hegel's view cannot, falsify the philosopher's claims to have provided a generally acceptable account of the way the world is.

There are, Hegel maintained, two mistakes which are often made in science and philosophy: one, which happens often in the modern period, is that "contingency has been unwarrantably elevated, and had a value attached

[5] *The Phenomenology of Mind*, pp. 254–255.

to it, both in nature and the world of mind, to which it has no just claim"; the other mistake occurs when we are "misled by a well-meant endeavor after rational knowledge" and "try to exhibit the necessity of phenomena which are marked by a decided contingency, or . . . to construe them *a priori*." [6] For Hegel the basic problem can be stated as follows: how to give contingency its proper due while recognizing that for science and philosophy contingency must in a sense be overcome? "The problem of science, and especially of philosophy," Hegel wrote, "undoubtedly consists in eliciting the necessity concealed under the semblance of contingency. That however is far from meaning that the contingent belongs to our subjective conception alone, and must therefore be simply set aside, if we wish to get at the truth." [7]

Instead of being a merely subjective conception, contingency, according to Hegel, occurs both in nature and in the world of mind. Those who admire nature for the richness and variety of its structures and who see contingency in this richness and variety are not mistaken— as evidence of such contingency Hegel himself cites "the chequered scene" presented by several varieties of animals and plants and "the complex changes in the figuration and groupings of clouds." But he writes that the wonderment with which such phenomena are noted is "a most abstract frame of mind, from which one should advance to a closer insight into the inner harmony and

[6] *The Logic of Hegel,* pp. 263, 265.   [7] *Ibid.,* p. 265.

uniformity of nature." In the mental realm Hegel maintains that contingency takes the form of option or freedom of the will. But while admitting that freedom of choice, or "the capacity of determining ourselves towards one thing or another," is a vital element in the will Hegel cautions against exaggerating its importance. "The genuinely free will," he writes, "which includes free choice as suspended, is conscious to itself that its content is firm and fast, and knows it at the same time to be thoroughly its own. A will, on the contrary, which remains standing on the grade of option, even supposing it does decide in favour of what is in import right and true, is always haunted by the conceit that it might, if it had so pleased, have decided in favour of the reverse course." [8] In writing about how the genuinely free will suspends free choice and is conscious that its content is "firm and fast," Hegel is, I believe, thinking of how contingency can be overcome by a necessity which in this case is both moral and practical. On this view doing involves deliberation and choice, but once alternative courses of action have been considered and a choice has been made the will, if it is to be "genuinely" (substantively rather than merely formally) free, must abide by the choice it has made. A preoccupation with contingency, with one's freedom to do otherwise, is from both the moral and the practical points of view harmful: it can prevent one's acting at all or it can adversely affect

[8] *Ibid.*, p. 264.

the resolve with which one seeks to bring about certain
results. In both the world of nature and the world of
mind an abstract marvelling over richness and variety
can stand in the way of "a closer insight" into the order
and uniformity of most, though not all, phenomena, and
in cases where this happens we have, according to Hegel,
given to contingency more than its proper due.

Hegel's answer to the question of how philosophy
conceives of contingency and necessity occurs mainly in
the context of an analysis of actuality. Here Hegel distinguishes between three stages: he treats first, "Contingency, or Formal Actuality, Possibility, and Necessity,"
second, "Relative Necessity, or Real Actuality, Possibility, and Necessity," and third, "Absolute Necessity." He
then considers, "The Relation of Substantiality," "The
Relation of Causality," and "Reciprocity," these three
relations being examples of "Necessity." Rather than
undertake a comprehensive analysis of Hegel's discussion of these topics in the *Science of Logic* and the *Encyclopedia* I shall attempt to describe briefly certain aspects of his treatment of contingency, relative or real
necessity, and absolute necessity so that we may have a
reliable general picture of how, according to Hegel, philosophy marks the relationship between contingency and
necessity.

Hegel defines actuality as the unity of essence with
existence, or of inward with outward. Actuality is first

of all possibility: "What is actual is possible." [9] But possibility is merely formal possibility—"the rule for it merely is that a thing must not be self-contradictory." [10] We are at first thought disposed to see possibility as a richer and more comprehensive category than actuality, but Hegel believes that reflection will show that merely the formal predication '*it is possible*' is superficial and empty: "*A is possible* means only that *A is A*." [11] It is possible, Hegel observes contemptuously, that the Sultan may become Pope, that being a man he may convert to Christianity, may become a priest, and so on. Everything, on this view, becomes possible for which you can state some ground or reason, but by the same token everything becomes impossible as well. How far then can possibility be said to be actuality? Everything possible has a being or an existence, but merely formal possibility is only formal actuality: "This unity of possibility and actuality is contingency. The contingent is an actual that at the same time is determined as merely possible, whose other or opposite equally is. This actuality is therefore mere being or Existence, but posited in its truth as having the value of a positedness or of possibility." Contingency is ultimately an unsatisfactory concept because it is such an unsatisfactory union of possibility and actuality. Hegel speaks of the "*absolute*

[9] *Hegel's Science of Logic*, p. 542.
[10] *The Logic of Hegel*, p. 260.
[11] *Hegel's Science of Logic*, p. 543.

unrest" of possibility and actuality in contingency: "But just because each immediately turns into its opposite, equally in this other it simply *unites with itself,* and this identity of both, of one in the other, is necessity." [12] Necessity, however, remains merely formal so long as its moments, possibility and actuality, are formal.

Formal actuality, formal possibility, and formal necessity would be of little or no interest to Hegel as abstract categories were it not the case that there is in the world real actuality, real possibility, and real necessity. Formal possibility possessed no content, no determinateness; it consisted solely in the absence of contradiction. With real possibility this is no longer the case: "Under formal possibility, because something was possible, then—not *itself*—but its *other* was also possible. Real possibility no longer has over against it *such an other,* for it is itself also actuality." What is necessary *"cannot be otherwise;* but what is simply [formally] *possible* can." Hegel then maintains that real possibility is necessity: "real possibility, because it contains the other moment, actuality, is already itself necessity. Therefore what is really possible cannot be otherwise; under the particular conditions and circumstances something else cannot follow. Real possibility and necessity are therefore only seemingly different; this is an identity which does not have to *become* but is already *presupposed* and lies at their base." [13]

The quotation above is troublesome in that on first

[12] *Ibid.,* p. 545.   [13] *Ibid.,* p. 549.

reading it seems to support the view which insists that in Hegel's system there is no room for genuine contingency. Formal possibility, on such an interpretation, tells us nothing about the real world, and real possibility, according to Hegel, only *seems* to differ from necessity but is actually identical with it. In short, there are only two states of affairs allowed for by Hegel which are relevant here: either a thing is merely formally possible or it is necessary. However, this must be false because there are things in the world which are real possibilities but not all of which are ever actualized and which therefore cannot be characterized as necessary save in a thoroughly misleading way. This argument is designed to call our attention to a third state of affairs, that besides formal possibility and necessity there is real possibility which, contrary to Hegel, *can* be otherwise. But whether Hegel has actually slighted or denied this third alternative depends ultimately upon what sense should be given to 'a real possibility which can be otherwise' and whether Hegel could do justice to this sense without abandoning his claim that real possibility and real necessity nevertheless turn out to be identical.

If Hegel's critic is willing to accept Hegel's example of the Sultan's becoming the Pope as an example of merely formal possibility, what would he accept as an example of a real possibility which can be otherwise? Perhaps the Sultan's becoming a scientist might suffice: let us imagine that the Sultan has a keen intellect, that his religion does nothing to discourage an interest in science, that there is in his kingdom a community of scientists with whom he is on good terms, that the Sultan wants to become a scientist, that his country is prosperous and at peace, and that the affairs of state are in the hands of an able and loyal minister. Such a story would seem to support, very strongly, the claim that the Sultan will in time become a scientist, but then he may not: he may be distracted by a new face in the harem or a neighboring kingdom may unexpectedly declare war. This is, therefore, an acceptable example, Hegel's critic might allow, of a real possibility which can be otherwise. (He may also add tartly that one need not turn to "fiction" for such examples, for real possibilities which can be, and often are, otherwise are "the very stuff" of which history is made.) But is such a counterexample fatal to Hegel's claim that what is really possible and what is necessary are identical? Or is it a counterexample at all?

At this juncture it is important to recall that immediately following his claim that what is really possible cannot be otherwise Hegel added that "under the particular conditions and circumstances something else cannot follow." This emphasis upon "particular conditions and circumstances" may be construed as Hegel's way of insisting upon the importance of the search for what is sometimes referred to, more precisely, as the necessary and sufficient conditions for the occurrence of a given phenomenon. If applied to our example of the Sultan's becoming a scientist, Hegel's emphasis upon "particular conditions and circumstances" would yield the following result: what we are saying is that if the Sultan has the intelligence and the desire to become a scientist, if his religious convictions do not stand in the way, and if he is not distracted by affairs of state or of the heart, then he will become a scientist. There are, of course, many complex philosophical problems which would require detailed attention in a comprehensive analysis of the issues posed by our example, most of them having to do with the difficult problem of counterfactuals. We should also have to consider the suggestion that the crucial consideration in cases of this kind does not involve empirical laws about how certain kinds of agents behave nor law-like statements about how a particular agent behaves, but rather analytic statements about concepts such as 'desiring' and 'wanting': is it analytically true, for example, that, other things being equal, a man who wants to x will x? [14] However these issues may be resolved, Hegel should be read as having reminded us that when we have correctly ascertained "the particular conditions and circumstances" for the occurrence of a given phenomenon and have noted moreover that these conditions do obtain, then we expect, rightly enough, that phe-

[14] See Alan Donagan, *The Later Philosophy of R. G. Collingwood* (Oxford, 1962), pp. 182–192.

nomenon to occur, and in that very strong sense marked by Hegel's "something else cannot follow."

The advocate of a real possibility which can be otherwise may, however, want to argue that nothing in the brief theoretical remarks I have just made explains the very real possibility that the Sultan may not become a scientist. To this one need only reply that if the Sultan does not become a scientist one must try to ascertain which of "the particular conditions and circumstances" for his becoming a scientist failed to obtain. Here the defender of "real possibility" might respond that this just pushes the search for the really possible one step further: for example, it may now turn out that it was the coming of war and not the Sultan's becoming a scientist which could have been otherwise. But this, while it may tell us how a given line of inquiry might actually proceed as we try to explain the war which is alleged to explain the Sultan's failure to become a scientist, can be in other respects only a misunderstanding. For both the Sultan's failure to become a scientist (as our example now reads) and the coming of war are real possibilities and hence real necessities. The Sultan's failure to become a scientist and the coming of war are real possibilities in the sense that under certain conditions these things would have occurred but that under other conditions they would not have occurred; and they are necessary in the sense that in the presence of certain conditions they could not have failed to occur. If, to return our example to its original form, the Sultan did after all become a scientist even though for a time there was a real possibility that he would not what this means is that one set of conditions prevailed in the world at a given time while another did not. I should argue that this picture of possibility and necessity is far removed from being hostile to what goes on in empirical investigations and is, so far as I can judge, compatible with any *ordinary* sense of 'a real possibility which *can* be otherwise.'

Part of the reason why Hegel's picture of possibility and necessity seems, at this point at least, so unexceptional is that the necessity in question is a "relative" necessity, meaning that the occurrence of an event such as the Sultan's becoming a scientist is necessary only in relation to the occurrence or existence of a given set of conditions and circumstances—the relation being marked here is one of dependence, and a necessity which is dependent can only be a relative necessity. Relative or real necessity has its "presupposition" or "starting point" in the contingent, and the really necessary is defined as "any limited actuality which, on account of this limitation, is also only a *contingent* in some other respect." [15]

Real necessity is a determinate necessity, according to Hegel, and the determinateness of necessity "consists in its containing its negation, contingency, within itself." Necessity not only contains contingency implicitly within itself but contingency "becomes" in it and this

[15] *Hegel's Science of Logic*, pp. 549, 550.

becoming is also necessity's becoming.[16] For the immediate becoming of the contingent provides the occasion for the becoming of necessity. The contingent is, as Findlay observes, the necessary condition of the necessary.[17] In necessity contingency is overcome not in the sense of being annulled or destroyed but in Hegel's special sense of being "sublated." "It is therefore necessity itself which determines itself as contingency—in its being repels itself from itself and in this very repulsion has only returned into itself, and in this return, as its being, has repelled itself from itself." [18]

Absolute necessity is, Hegel writes, the truth into which actuality and possibility and formal and real necessity "withdraw": "It is as much simple immediacy or *pure being* as simple reflection-into-self or *pure essence;* it is this, that these two are one and the same. That which is simply necessary only *is* because it *is;* it has neither condition nor ground. But equally it is pure *essence;* its being is simple reflection-into-self; it is, *because* it is." Absolute necessity is further "the *reflection or form of the absolute*": on the one hand, its differences do not have "the shape of the determinations of reflection, but of *a simply affirmative multiplicity*, a differentiated ac-

[16] *Ibid.*, p. 551.

[17] Findlay, *op. cit.*, p. 213. See also *"Hegels Theorie über den Zufall"* by Dieter Henrich, *Kant-Studien*, L (1958–59), pp. 131–148; *"Nur wenn es ein absolut Zuffäliges gibt, ist Notwendigkeit denkbar,"* p. 135.

[18] *Hegel's Science of Logic*, p. 551.

tuality which has the shape of others, self-subsistent rela-
tively to one another"; on the other hand, its relation is
absolute identity, the absolute conversion of its actuality
into its possibility and of its possibility into actuality.
This is why, according to Hegel, absolute necessity is
"blind." The various things which go to make up the
world appear as "*free actualities*, neither of which is reflected in the other, nor will let any trace of its relation
to the other show in it; grounded in itself, each is the
necessary in its own self. Necessity as *essence* is concealed in this *being;* contact between these actualities
appears therefore as an empty externality, the actuality
of the one in the other is *only* possibility, contingency.
. . . But this contingency is rather absolute necessity;
it is the *essence* of those free, inherently necessary actualities. This essence is *light-shy*. . . . But their *essence*
will break forth in them and reveal what *it* is and what
they are." [19] The metaphors of necessity conceived of as
"blind" and of the essence of actualities conceived of as
"light-shy" serve to convey Hegel's belief that the necessity of relationships which on one level appear to be
merely external will yield itself up only to the most systematic and laborious investigations. But it is the essential task of inquiry to show that the things in the world
are moments that constitute a totality which is itself "necessity—being, simply and solely as reflection." [20]

[19] *Ibid.*, pp. 552–553.　　[20] *Ibid.*, p. 554.

A Teleological Explanation of the "Whole" of History

If human inquiry is to succeed in showing that the things in the world are necessarily interrelated, some division of labor will be required among philosophy and the various empirical sciences. One could, of course, argue that the tasks of philosophy and the natural sciences, for example, are too disparate for us to speak significantly of a division of labor in this connection, that philosophy has as its subject matter the infinite while the natural sciences have as their subject matter only finite objects, and that where the objects of inquiry differ so greatly any talk about the division of labor in this connection is artificial and misleading. But this would, I think, make too much of the infinite-finite distinction in Hegel, and it would not be easily applicable, as I have argued, to an empirical science or discipline such as history whose objects of inquiry, concerning as they do human consciousness, have both finite and infinite aspects. Moreover, Hegel gives us reason to suppose that he believed empirical investigations can confirm, in the sense of providing supporting evidence for, at least some philosophical hypotheses, especially those which are in effect philosophical interpretations of the findings of the natural sciences and of history. Otherwise it is difficult to see why he would have bothered to do philosophy of nature and philosophy of history in the ways he did, with careful attention to the findings of scientists and historians. And if Hegel did believe in the empirical confirmation of some philosophical hypotheses, such a belief would make little or no sense if one attached an exaggerated significance to differences between the objects of philosophical inquiry and of scientific investigation.[21]

If, however, we grant that philosophy and the empirical sciences do in some sense share the same subject matter, let it be called informally the world in general, and that some division of labor is required to show the necessary interrelations of the things in this world, it does not, of course, follow that every empirical science will be able to contribute to Hegel's project. It might turn out that some empirical sciences have as their subject matter objects which remain recalcitrantly, irredeem-

[21] My claim that Hegel believed empirical investigations can confirm, in the sense of providing supporting evidence for, some philosophical hypotheses is supported by the following quotation from *The Philosophy of Nature:* "Not only must philosophy be in agreement with our empirical knowledge of Nature, but the *origin* and *formation* of the Philosophy of Nature presupposes and is conditioned by empirical physics." However, my claim must be qualified by what Hegel says in the next paragraph. Here Hegel maintains that *philosophical* knowledge must give an account of the object as determined by its Concept, although we must also "name" the empirical appearance corresponding to it and must also show that the empirical appearance does, in fact, correspond to the Concept: "However, this is not an appeal to experience in regard to the necessity of the content" (*Hegel's Philosophy of Nature*, translated by A. V. Miller [Oxford, 1970], pp. 6–7).

ably "light-shy," resisting all efforts to reveal their interrelations. How would such a possibility affect Hegel's
position?

First we must raise the question of how a science
could possibily fail to lend any support to the claim that
the things in the world are in Hegel's sense necessarily
interrelated and mutually conditioning, which I shall call
Hegel's Necessitarian Hypothesis. If I read Hegel correctly in this regard, the establishment of any scientific
hypothesis or law must lend some support to Hegel's
Necessitarian Hypothesis, for such an hypothesis or law,
ideally at any rate, tells us that under certain kinds of
conditions certain kinds of phenomena will occur. In
other words every success of science in subsuming phenomena under laws supports to some degree the philosophical interpretation of necessity provided by Hegel,
especially in his remarks concerning relative or real necessity. But let us suppose that an empirical science fails
to establish one or more of its hypotheses. What bearing
would this have upon Hegel's position? While Hegel believed, I think, in the empirical confirmation of some
philosophical hypotheses, his position concerning the
question of the empirical disconfirmation or falsification
of philosophical hypotheses is more complex. Although
he wrote in *The Philosophy of Nature* that "philosophy
must be in agreement with our empirical knowledge of
Nature," he also wrote that what is known through the
Concept (through philosophical analysis of the Con-

cept) "is clear by itself and stands firm; and philosophy need not feel any embarrassment about this, even if all phenomena are not yet explained." Here Hegel notes a contrast between philosophy and the "finite sciences": "In these sciences, the sole verification of the hypothesis lies in the empirical element and everything must be explained." [22] What Hegel intends by these remarks is, I think, the following: the confirmation of philosophical hypotheses about nature (and history) can be thought of as taking place on two levels, the philosophical and the empirical, while the confirmation of scientific hypotheses takes place solely on the empirical level. Philosophical hypotheses must be "in agreement with our empirical knowledge"; and in Chapter One we traced Hegel's efforts to prove that philosophical history was not a priori in the sense of being a merely speculative enterprise conceived without a proper respect for factual or empirical considerations. However, philosophical hypotheses need only be in *general* agreement with our empirical knowledge and are not to be considered as disconfirmed "even if all phenomena are not yet explained," while scientific hypotheses must be in *complete* agreement with the "empirical element"—"everything must be explained." If we accept this disanalogy between philosophy and the empirical sciences on the question of hypothesis disconfirmation or falsification, the failure of some empirical science on one or more occasions to sup-

[22] *Ibid.*, p. 82.

ply support for Hegel's Necessitarian Hypothesis would not adversely affect that hypothesis.

However, let us imagine a case where a science never successfully confirms even one of its hypotheses. This cannot, I believe, damage Hegel's Necessitarian Hypothesis, for all it can do is to show, over a period of time, that the science in question is not really a science. Hegel explicitly, and rightly, denies that a mere collection of facts can count as a science. In other words, a science lacking successful hypotheses, laws, or explanations is nothing but a collection of facts (of answers perhaps to what or how questions but not to why questions), and thus such a science is not, strictly speaking, a science at all. Of course, not all empirical knowledge is scientific knowledge, and in some cases we might find ourselves left with a body of empirical knowledge about the formation of clouds or the caprices of the mind, to use two of Hegel's examples, which can count only as a collection of data and not as a science.

But would it be correct to speak of Hegel's examples of the formation of clouds or the caprices of the mind as "examples of superficial Contingency, for which it would be wrong to seek a necessitating explanation?" [23] This question is not easy to answer on Hegel's behalf: if we say yes, then we seem to be legislating as philosophers for scientists, thus setting a priori limits to what the science of meteorology or the science of psychology

[23] Findlay, *op. cit.*, p. 212.

can do; if we answer no, then we must be prepared to deny that there may be kinds of phenomena not amenable to a necessitating explanation. I shall try to formulate a general solution to this problem, but I shall do so by exploring the possibility that history is a paradigm of an empirical science or a data-collecting discipline which has as its subject matter objects, namely human beings and their actions, which are by their very nature "light-shy" and for which it would be wrong to seek a necessitating explanation.

In the Preface to the *Phenomenology* Hegel wrote: "Regarding historical truths—to mention these briefly— insofar as their purely historical aspect is considered, it will be readily granted that they concern particular existence and the accidental and arbitrary side, the features that are not necessary." [24]

Walter Kaufmann has remarked that this brief passage shows the popular notion of Hegel's philosophy of history, that historical events are necessary and can be deduced a priori, to be "utterly wrong." [25] Of course, it might be objected that this is perhaps to attach too much importance to a brief observation made by Hegel in his first book, but the *Phenomenology* was in no sense a youthful work and the emphasis upon the accidental and arbitrary nature of historical events is to be found

[24] Translated by Walter Kaufmann, *Hegel*, p. 416.
[25] *Ibid.*, p. 417.

throughout Hegel's works. In *The Philosophy of Right*, for example, he writes that "the state is no ideal work of art; it stands on earth and so in the sphere of caprice, chance, and error, and bad behaviour may disfigure it in many respects." [26]

If in the above quotations, one takes 'accidental,' 'arbitrary,' 'caprice,' 'chance,' and 'error' to stand for 'contingency,' it would be difficult to see how the notion that Hegel neglected the role of contingency in human history ever took hold. Instead the above passages suggest that Hegel may have in effect put the events of human history on a par with the formation of clouds and the caprices of the mind, as exhibiting a contingency for which it would be if not altogether wrong then surely unprofitable or fruitless to seek a "necessitating explanation." And if Hegel did so regard historical events, he is not alone in this: when some professional historians, in their "philosophical" moments, speak of history as "a rope of sand" or as "one damn thing after another," or when they speculate about how different history might have been if only the length of Cleopatra's nose had been different they seem to be in effect endorsing Hegel's view that historical truths "concern particular existence and the accidental and arbitrary side, the features that are not necessary."

Yet the popular notion persists that Hegel did believe in historical necessity, and here, too, there is supporting

[26] Page 279.

evidence in the text. In *The Philosophy of History* he writes that "World history is the progress of the consciousness of freedom—a progress whose necessity we have to investigate," and he speaks of Spirit and not of accident, caprice, or chance as the "substance of history." [27] It has sometimes been suggested that when Hegel speaks of necessity in history he means thereby the 'rationally necessary,' that is to say merely the course which history would *ideally* follow if the processes of history were rational processes. Yet Hegel writes that "The rational, like the substantial, is necessary." [28] And he goes on to treat world history as being both a rational and a necessary process. "For world history is the manifestation of the Divine, the absolute process of Spirit in its highest forms. It is this development wherein it achieves its truth and the consciousness of itself." [29]

But how can history be said to be accidental and arbitrary and yet also rational and necessary? *Here it is vital to notice that it is "particular existence" that Hegel has in mind when he speaks of the accidental and arbitrary aspect of history and that it is "world history" or the entire historical process that he has in mind when considering the rational and necessary aspect of history.* In this connection it should be noticed that 'particular' and 'particularity' function as technical terms in Hegel's philosophy and that, as the following quotation illus-

[27] *Reason in History*, pp. 24, 20.   [28] *Ibid.*, p. 53.
[29] *Ibid.*, p. 67.

trates, they are especially apt in helping to mark the distinction betwen the contingent and the necessary aspects of history:

The state in its actuality is essentially an individual state, and beyond that a particular state. Individuality is to be distinguished from particularity. The former is a moment in the very Idea of the state, while the latter belongs to history. States as such are independent of one another and therefore their relation to one another can only be an external one, so that there must be a third thing standing above them to bind them together. Now this third thing is the mind [Spirit] which gives itself actuality in world history and is the absolute judge of states.[30]

In the above individuality is contrasted with particularity at the expense of the latter. While individuality is a moment or element in the very Idea of the state, particularity belongs to history. Because states as such are independent of one another, their relation to one another is external, that is to say contingent, but Spirit binds these states together and actualizes itself in world history. In this case it is the activities of Spirit which provide the basis or ground for the necessitating explanation Hegel was seeking in his remarks about absolute necessity. States conceived of as particulars appear only as externally related, but conceived of as individuals they are necessarily related, each as an element of the Idea and each to be conceived of as an expression of the Spirit

[30] *The Philosophy of Right,* p. 279.

which actualizes itself in world history through these individual states.

Are the relations between states contingent or necessary? The answer to this question depends on whether the state is conceived of as a particular state externally related to other particular states or as an individual state necessarily bound to other individual states by virtue of the activities of Spirit. The basic point here is not simply that either answer is permissible, although this is so, but that the comprehension of the necessity of the relations between individual states takes place on a higher level of adequacy than does the comprehension of the contingency of the relations between particular states. By this I mean to suggest that on Hegel's view the comprehension of the contingency of the relations between particular states is "sublated" (preserved and yet transcended) in the comprehension of the necessity of the relations between individual states. Put in somewhat clearer terms, the comprehension of the contingency of the relations between particular states is a necessary condition, if I am applying Hegel's remarks about contingency and necessity correctly in this case, for the comprehension of the necessity of the relations between individual states, while the comprehension of the necessity of the relations between individual states is not a necessary condition for the comprehension of the contingency of the relations between particular states. The latter states simply *are*, although it can, of course, be said that it is logically conceivable they might be otherwise or might not *be* at all. But philosophy and history have this in common, that they have to start their investigations with the world as it is, in this case with the world of particular states. Since the state is according to Hegel the basic unit of historical study and thus also the starting point of philosophical interpretations of history, one can see that what we have said about the contingency and necessity of the relations between states is easily generalizable into a more comprehensive account of the roles of contingency and necessity in history.

One feature of Hegel's remarks concerning the particularity of historical entities and events is that he nowhere speaks of such entities and events as being merely or exclusively particular or contingent, but, perhaps of equal importance, he does not deny that some historical entities and events might be merely or exclusively contingent. It might be the case that some historical phenomena are on a par with cloud formations and mental caprices, are unyielding or "light-shy" in the face of our most persistent searches for a necessitating explanation. But would Hegel say that there is any natural class or set of historical phenomena that we can mark, in advance of further inquiries, as being so recalcitrant that it would be "wrong to seek a necessitating explanation" of them? In the final analysis and with the qualifications I have noted, Hegel in his treatment of mechanism and teleology did mark a certain class of phenomena, organic and spiritual objects, as not admitting of mechanical explanations; and in his discussion of causality he denied ultimately that causality as a category is applicable to the spiritual, or at least to the spiritual domain when the Spirit is actively present therein, but he went on to insist that the spiritual was properly explicable in teleological terms. Indeed I know of no class of phenomena for which he denied the possibility of necessitating explanations of some sort. In this connection I doubt whether the examples of cloud formations and mental caprices were ever intended by Hegel as more than examples of areas where no progress had been made in the search for necessitating explanation and where none seemed likely. But the unlikely is not to be confused with the impossible.

If we apply the above remarks to history, we are confronted with two principal results: (1) in cases where necessitating explanations are discovered, the discovery of necessity instead of annulling or cancelling out the presence of contingency acknowledges the presence of contingency in historical happenings; indeed, the discovery of necessity presupposes the presence rather than the absence of contingency; (2) in cases where necessitating explanations are not discovered, this does not prove either that historical phenomena in general or any subset thereof are in principle immune to any such discovery. Only the confused insistence upon the *particularity* of historical phenomena and the consequent refusal to see *individual* historical phenomena as elements of the Idea and as expressions of the activities of Spirit would lead one to believe that historical phenomena are merely or exclusively contingent; and Hegel's philosophy of history is aimed at providing a necessitating teleological explanation of the world historical process in terms of the ultimate purpose of the world.

There is a prevalent view to the effect that if even one historical phenomenon remains "light-shy" and refuses to yield to Hegel's teleological explanation, this would disconfirm or falsify Hegel's teleological explanation of the entire historical process. But Hegel at least believed that philosophy, unlike the empirical sciences, need not feel any embarrassment if it does not explain all phenomena. Perhaps the following example will help illustrate the sort of thing Hegel had in mind. The philosopher offers a necessitating explanation of world history as aiming at freedom, while the empirical historian seeks to establish a connection between life on the frontier and the growth of free political institutions. The historian may speak "naively" and say that the frontier causes the growth of free political institutions or, having read Hegel, he may say rather that the frontier provides the occasion or the external stimulus for the frontiersmen to decide that free political institutions are more in keeping with conditions of life on the frontier. Stated either way the historian's hypothesis is subject to empirical confirmation or disconfirmation, confirmation by the discovery of the growth of free political institutions on the frontier and disconfirmation by the discovery of the absence or the decline of free political institutions on the frontier. But the philosopher's necessitating explanation while it is partially confirmed by the success of the historian's hypothesis is not adversely affected by the failure of that hypothesis.

This, at least, is what Hegel would probably claim. I cannot here, in this attempted reconstruction of Hegel's position, undertake the detailed analysis it would require to justify or to dismiss Hegel's claim. However, one thing can be noted by way of partial defense, namely that the claim to be able to explain *any* whole does not logically depend upon the success or failure to explain each and every part or property of that whole. Here, somewhat surprisingly, we can turn to Karl Popper for some (unintended) support of Hegel's position. Popper notes the ambiguity of the word 'whole': "It is used to denote (*a*) the totality of all the properties or aspects of a thing, and especially of all the relations holding between its constituent parts, and (*b*) certain special properties or aspects of the thing in question, namely those which make it appear an organized structure, rather than a 'mere heap.'" Popper goes on to say that inquiry is necessarily selective (a point which Hegel anticipated when he indicated that history proceeds by abstraction) and that, therefore, "It is not possible for us to observe or describe a whole piece of the world, or a whole piece of nature" [31] where 'whole' is taken to denote the totality of all the properties or aspects of a thing, and especially of all the relations holding between its constituent parts. To be sure, Popper would in the present connection certainly wish to deny that 'the historical process' or 'world history' denotes any whole, would want to deny in other words that history is an organized structure rather than a mere heap of events; and partly as a result of this Popper would deny that it is legitimate to talk about the ultimate purpose of the world or of world history, or even the meaning of history, in any Hegelian sense.[32] However, Popper's main argument in the above quotations is supportive of Hegel in this way: no whole, no matter how small, can ever be known or described if we take 'whole' to denote all the properties or aspects of a thing and all the relations holding between its parts. Thus, *if we are to make any sense of Hegel's claim that he knows the whole of history, this claim must be construed as meaning that he knows certain properties, aspects, and relations of history, namely those which make it an organized structure.* In the light of this interpretation Hegel's claim that "I know the whole" of history and his further claim that "history itself must be taken as it is; we have to proceed historically, empirically" [33] can be

---

[31] *The Poverty of Historicism*, pp. 76–77.
[32] *The Open Society and Its Enemies*, pp. 443–463.
[33] *Reason in History*, p. 12.

read as follows. Hegel is not claiming to have any special extrahistorical vantage point from which he can survey the whole of the historical process, nor is he claiming what is logically impossible, namely that he can know the whole of history where 'whole' is taken to denote all the properties and relations of a thing. Rather Hegel is setting forth the hypothesis that world history is an organized structure, that is a structure possessing certain special properties or aspects, chiefly the property of being disposed toward the realization of an end state in which the freedom and self-consciousness of Spirit prevails. This hypothesis can be supported by empirical evidence that freedom is coming to prevail in the world, but it will not necessarily be disconfirmed or falsified by empirical evidence of some curtailments of freedom in the world. It will not necessarily be disconfirmed or falsified by such evidence because *it is legitimate to speak of certain properties or aspects of a thing as resulting in an organized structure of a certain kind, without thereby denying that there may be other properties or aspects of the thing in question which, if they ever became dominant, would make for a structure of quite a different kind.* (I would suppose that medicine is an area in which examples of this might easily be found: surely there are many cases in which properties making for good health and properties making for ill health exist alongside one another in the same body, but where the properties making for good health predominate over those making for ill health in such a way to justify the diagnosis that the body in question has a basically or fundamentally healthy structure.)

However, the question must be raised as to whether Hegel would want to make the stronger claim that no empirical evidence could possibly disconfirm or falsify his hypothesis that the whole of world history is a structure aimed at the realization of freedom. It is one thing to deny that the failure of any particular empirical hypothesis such as the one discussed in our "free political institutions on the frontier" example would render Hegel's hypothesis about the essential structure of world history either false or meaningless, but it would be far more serious to deny that a failure of all empirical inquiries to find *any* confirming evidence for Hegel's hypothesis could adversely affect that hypothesis. If Hegel in effect made such a denial, then he would, obviously, have to surrender his belief that this hypothesis is in general agreement with empirical findings and would have to admit that his philosophical history was merely speculative after all. Another way of putting the problem is this: while talk about history as having an "essential" structure aimed at the realization of freedom is compatible with the discovery of some "accidental" historical phenomena in which freedom is curtailed or denied, would it be compatible with a situation in which the "accidental" prevailed completely, a situation in which there would be no empirical evidence of freedom's existing anywhere or at any time in world history? Hegel might, I think, tentatively concede that in such a situation his hypothesis would be incompatible with the evidence and would have to be abandoned altogether or restated in drastically different terms. However, he would surely insist that in the light of our knowledge of the past and of the present such a situation is a very remote possibility, and he might wish to maintain moreover that a detailed description of such a situation would reveal a fundamental incoherence in the "possibility" we have posited. Besides the considerable empirical evidence that men *have* enjoyed varying degrees of freedom in history, there are certain conceptual tie-ins between 'history,' 'historical man,' and 'freedom' which our abstract statement of the possibility in question has ignored. History conceived of both as a discipline and as the subject matter of that discipline involves self-awareness, deliberation, and choice, which, if Hegel is correct, are necessarily related to freedom. Historical man is, however imperfectly, a free man in a way that prehistorical man is not. Thus to say that empirical studies of historical phenomena do not reveal the presence of any freedom in the historical process would be to strain and even violate concepts which are fundamental to our historical thinking. It would be to show that, literally, we don't know what we're talking about.

The Problem of Historical Explanation

In the preceding discussion I have spoken several times, using Findlay's phrase, of "necessitating explanations," and I wish to conclude this exploration of Hegel's philosophy of history by considering briefly and in a very general way what we now call "the problem of historical explanation" as this relates to Hegel.

But first a word of caution. An attempt to provide a sympathetic interpretation of Hegel (or any classical philosopher) inevitably runs the risk of modernizing unduly his position in a number of ways, some conscious and others unconscious. One of the greatest risks occurs when one is tempted to recast his argument or to restate his position in the language our contemporaries use in discussing the "same" philosophical issue. Thus, we might be tempted to treat Hegel's distinction between the empirical and the a priori as being in effect a distinction between the empirical investigation of phenomena and the philosophical analysis of concepts, and to assume that Hegel means by the philosophical analysis of concepts exactly what we do. Or we might try to assimilate Hegel's discussion of mechanism and teleology to the language used in the debate in our time between mechanists and vitalists and to assume that Hegel in talking about the problem of whether mechanism is "sublated" in teleology is at least in part discussing the question of whether mechanical laws are "reducible" to teleological ones or vice versa. Finally, where Hegel's philosophy of history is concerned there is the temptation to treat Hegel as if he were a participant in the "covering law" controversy about the nature of historical explanation which is current in our time among analytical philosophers of history; but this is such an attractive temptation, and provided one knows that one is sinning the results may prove instructive.

In Chapter One I argued that Hegel did not intend to provide us with even the outlines of a predictive science of history, and that his teleological approach to history was essentially retrospective in nature. In the section above I have argued that while Hegel believed the empirical sciences could confirm, in the sense of supplying supporting evidence for, philosophical hypotheses about nature or history, Hegel did not believe such philosophical hypotheses could be disconfirmed or falsified by their failure to explain *all* phenomena.[34] Taken together, these two arguments suggest how Hegel's teleological interpretation of history could escape from being harmed by two separate but related theses about the nature of *scientific* explanation that are current in some contemporary philosophical circles. The first thesis stated simply maintains that any scientifically acceptable explanation must be symmetrical in form with scientific predictions

[34] "The universal law is not designed for individuals as such, who indeed may find themselves very much the losers. . . . In affirming . . . that the universal Reason *does* actualize itself, we have nothing to do with the empirical detail. For this can be better or worse; here chance and particularity have received authority to exercise their tremendous power. Much fault, therefore, might be found in phenomenal details" (*Reason in History*, pp. 46–47).

and must be the sort of thing which in principle could itself serve as a prediction. Proponents of this thesis concede that in practice, owing to lack of information at the relevant time or to the level of development in a given science, many explanations may fail to satisfy such a requirement, but such explanations should be construed either as "explanation sketches" or in some cases as "pseudo-explanations." [35] The second thesis maintains that a teleological explanation is scientifically acceptable only if it is in principle reducible to a mechanical one, that is to an explanation in terms of efficient causation. Again it is conceded that in practice, owing to lack of information or the level of development in a given science, this requirement may not be satisfied by many teleological explanations. Thus, in biology, the social sciences, and history one may encounter explanations stated

[35] See Carl G. Hempel, "The Function of General Laws in History," *Aspects of Scientific Explanation* (New York, 1965), pp. 231–243. Hempel dismisses historical explanation in terms of the " 'self-unfolding of absolute reason' " because the concepts used in this explanation are "mere metaphors without cognitive content" (p. 237). According to Hempel, a scientific explanation of an event E consists of "(1) a set of statements asserting the occurrence of certain events $C_1 \ldots C_n$ at certain times and places, (2) a set of universal hypotheses, such that (a) the statements of both groups are reasonably well confirmed by empirical evidence, (b) from the two groups of statements the sentence asserting the occurrence of event E can be logically deduced" (p. 232). It should perhaps be emphasized that the deductive necessity in the above concerns the relations between *statements* and not between events.

in terms of goals or end states. But to the extent that such explanations imply that future states of affairs determine present or past states of affairs they are unacceptable. For example, Dave Lewis' purchase of a Ferrari in 1969 cannot be said to have determined his behavior in the stock market in 1968, but his desire in 1968 to purchase a Ferrari in 1969 can be said to causally explain his behavior in the market in 1968.[36]

In the course of this study I have not discussed the first thesis in any detail and I have not mentioned the second thesis at all before undertaking these concluding remarks, chiefly because I believe the presuppositions and philosophical perspectives of Hegel and the advocates of one or both of these theses differ so greatly that it is doubtful whether a systematic comparison of Hegel's position with theirs would illuminate to any great extent what Hegel was trying to do. But by way of a conclusion some general remarks may now be ventured. First, to the extent that Hegel regarded his teleological explanations of nature and history as nonscientific and "philosophical" his claims would presumably be of no direct concern to positivists and mechanists. And I know of no philosophical refutation of the claim that nonscientific or philosophical interpretations of the world can be supported by empirical evidence, even when this evi-

[36] See especially the papers by Richard D. Braithwaite, Ernest Nagel, and Carl G. Hempel in *Purpose in Nature*, edited by John V. Canfield (Englewood Cliffs, 1966).

dence is supplied by the empirical sciences. While Hegel seems to have believed that evidence supplied by the empirical sciences can support at least some philosophical hypotheses, he did not believe that philosophy can confirm or disconfirm any scientific hypotheses, and this willing recognition on Hegel's part of the autonomy of science should help convince positivists and mechanists that they have no direct quarrel with Hegel on this issue. So long as Hegel's teleological explanations, interpretations, or hypotheses are not covertly causal in their content, Hegel and the positivists and mechanists can pass without touching.

However, an eventual collision is unavoidable where the question of the adequacy of scientific explanation as a way of looking at the world is concerned. Yet here there is an agreement before there is a difference: unlike ordinary-language philosophers, who are chiefly concerned with noting and describing different senses of 'explain,' Hegel and the positivists and mechanists wish to put forth in effect a philosophical *theory* of what will count as an adequate or complete explanation of natural and historical phenomena. Speaking somewhat schematically, one can say that for the positivist and mechanist this requirement of adequacy or completeness is satisfied when such phenomena are subsumed under scientific laws, while for Hegel the answer to the question of what kind or kinds of things will count as a necessitating explanation is twofold. For Hegel either a mechanical, causal explanation or a teleological explanation can count as a necessitating explanation; but as I showed in Chapter Two it is the mechanical, causal explanation which Hegel views as ultimately incomplete and which is to be "sublated" (but not reduced) in teleological explanation. As a *description* of what goes on in the sciences a positivist-mechanist account seems in one important respect acceptable to Hegel: when the scientist shows that under certain conditions certain phenomena will occur he is providing a necessitating explanation that would seem to satisfy the requirements set forth in Hegel's discussion of real or relative necessity. Yet Hegel, from the philosophical perspective, questions and ultimately rejects the adequacy or completeness of scientific explanation.

In the *Phenomenology* in his analysis of how we move from sense-certainty to perceptual consciousness and to scientific understanding, Hegel clearly regards this movement as progressive. Nevertheless his strictures concerning scientific understanding are severe. Scientific understanding, according to Hegel, mistakes unconditioned universals for nonphenomenal objects or realities and speaks of the latter as forces which it seeks to explain by laws. Such laws, however, err in either the direction of having no empirical content and have simply the bare concept of law, as Hegel believes is true of most general laws, or in the direction of simply redescribing at the more particular level the phenomena they purport to explain. Such an explanation is "tautological" or an explanation which "explains nothing." [37] In the *Science of Logic* Hegel repeats his charge that explanation in terms of scientific laws is "tautological." [38] The ultimate basis for this charge lies, I think, in Hegel's belief that propositions about the cause-effect relation are "tautological": "Rain, for example, is the cause of wetness which is its effect; the rain wets—this is an analytic proposition." [39] If propositions about causal relations are "tautological," and if such propositions take the form of causal laws, then explanation of natural phenomena in terms of such laws will be "tautological."

I believe that none of the above claims made by Hegel would be acceptable to philosophers of science today. The confusion of forces with laws of which Hegel makes so much in his critique of scientific understanding is simply a confusion which can readily be identified as such when it occurs, for laws are statements which explain the operations of forces and forces are never properly spoken of as laws. "Laws" which have no empirical content and have only the bare concept of law are in no sense laws but only the form which the statement of laws takes. If I say 'all *x*'s are *y*'s' or 'if *x*, then *y*' but refuse to provide any specifiable content for '*x*' or '*y*', I have not provided anyone with a scientific law. If, on the other hand, my "law" simply redescribes the phenomena it purports to explain, this "law" is no explanation. If

[37] *Phenomenology of Mind*, pp. 178–201.
[38] *Hegel's Science of Logic*, p. 714.   [39] *Ibid.*, p. 516.

the redescription is "tautological" or "analytic" and Hegel here uses these terms interchangeably, it isn't properly speaking a redescription of an empirical phenomenon but the statement of a conceptual truth. But if 'rain
wets' is analytic 'rain wets the streets' is not. 'Rain wets
the streets' is an explanation or a low level law in which
what might be called, if Hegel wants, "a force," namely
rain, is said to have caused the wetness of the streets.

Long argument would, of course, be required to sus-
tain any one of the above responses to Hegel which I
have made, but if I am correct in saying that there is
nothing or virtually nothing of merit in Hegel's strictures concerning scientific explanation and that indeed
these strictures appear to constitute an Achilles' heel for
Hegel's system, then the question must be put, Why
did a philosopher of Hegel's unusual acumen turn in
such a bad performance on this occasion? The answer
lies, I believe, chiefly in Hegel's haste to underscore the
limits of scientific understanding in general, and the reason for this haste lies in the fact that Hegel has an alternative to the positivist-mechanist theory as to what can
count as a fully adequate or complete explanation of natural and historical phenomena.

Hegel's theory, unlike that of the positivist and mechanist, rests ultimately not upon an analysis of the logic
of explanation in the various sciences which investigate
the objects in the world but upon differences in the
kinds of objects which there are in the world. At any

rate, I shall try to show that Hegel's is a metaphysical, or if that word offends, an ontological theory for evaluating the adequacy or completeness of explanations. It should also be noted that Hegel's "theory," although he does not explicitly offer it as such or explicitly make the following point in its defense, is a reflection of what might be spoken of as the classical Aristotelian belief or prejudice to the effect that A does not adequately explain B if A itself is in need of some further explanation or if B can be explained by anything other than A. That Hegel had this belief or something very much like it in mind is evident from his discussion of mechanism and the relation of mechanical objects to one another. In Chapter Two we explored Hegel's belief that mechanical objects are mutually indifferent, are neither attracted to nor repelled by one another. Thus, Hegel reasoned, any mechanical object can equally well function as the cause or the effect of any other mechanical object. There is, accordingly, no "natural" or ontologically justified place in mechanical investigations to which we can point as a terminus to mechanical explanation, no place at which we can rest satisfied that now our explanation is fully adequate or complete.

It was, I think, largely because of this alleged deficiency in mechanical objects that Hegel doubted the sufficiency of mechanical explanation. This interpretation is supported by the following passage where Hegel argues that mechanical determinism "can halt and be satisfied at any point at will, because the object it has reached in its progress, being a formal totality, is shut up within itself and indifferent to its being determined by another. Consequently, the *explanation* of the determination of an object and the progressive determining of the object made for the purpose of the explanation, is only an *empty word*, since in the other object to which it advances there resides no self-determination. Now as the determinateness of an object *lies in another*, no determinate difference is to be found between them, the determinateness is merely doubled, once in one object and again in the other, something utterly *identical*, so that the explanation or comprehension is tautological." [40]

[40] *Ibid.*, p. 714. This quotation poses the problem of whether we should continue to speak of mechanical explanation as a *kind* of necessitating explanation in Hegel. However, I think we should do so on two grounds: (1) Hegel's argument in this quotation is overstated and does not, and cannot, prove what Hegel thinks it does. Where two objects are causally related it does not follow from the fact that either object could equally well serve as the cause or the effect of the other *on different occasions* that no other significant difference obtains between the two objects and that, therefore, the determinateness of one by the other *on any given occasion* would be a matter of "identity" with the result that the causal explanation of this determinateness would be "tautological." If billiard ball A strikes billiard ball B thus causing it to move, the adequacy of the explanation that billiard ball B moved because it was struck by billiard ball A is in no way affected by the resemblances of the two billiard balls to one another, by their mutual "indifference" to one another, or by the fact that it is possible that on another occasion billiard ball B might strike billiard ball A thus causing

Scientific understanding as this operates in mechanism (chemism, it should be recalled, allows for mutual attraction and repulsion on the part of its objects) deals with objects that are causally determined by other objects; and any explanation of the relationship between these objects is bound, Hegel believes, to reflect the deficiency or limits he has noted in these objects. *Adequate or complete explanations on this view are of objects which do not require explanation in terms of their being causally determined by other objects. Ontologically adequate objects are self-determining ones and the proper explanation of such objects is teleological not causal.*

What are the ontologically adequate objects that are the subject matter for fully adequate or complete explanations? The answer is that men insofar as the spiritual aspect predominates over the physical aspect of their nature are such objects. How can the explanation of these objects and their actions be teleological? The

it to move. What is logically possible, as Hegel reminds us elsewhere, is not to be confused with what is really possible in any given situation. (2) Hegel speaks of mechanism as being sublated in teleology and of teleology's utilizing mechanism's empirical understanding of how objects causally relate to one another. But if all mechanical explanation could provide is a series of tautologies it is impossible to see what use it could be to teleology or even to the mechanical sciences. Thus, I regard Hegel's criticism of mechanical explanation in the above as being a misapplication of his ontological analysis of the inadequacy of the *objects* studied by mechanism.

answer here is twofold: first, men as historical (self-aware) agents pursue certain subjective ends which they seek to realize in the world [41]; second, the interactions of such agents with one another and with the world of nature serve to bring about a final or ultimate end of which these agents are largely or wholly unaware, which is the freedom and self-consciousness of Spirit. The explanation of the actions of individual agents is teleological, but not entirely so because while such agents are self-determining they are not entirely so: their actions are limited by those of other men, as well as by social institutions and physical conditions. However, since according to Hegel the world historical process in which human actions occur is entirely self-determining (and mechanical determinations within this process are sublated in teleological ones) the explanation of this process can in the final analysis be entirely teleological. Moreover *the final or ultimate end (what Hegel calls "the ultimate purpose") in which this process is to be explained is itself susceptible to no further explanation;* and

[41] Carl G. Hempel reminds us that it is, strictly speaking, a misnomer to speak of the teleological explanation of human actions in terms of an agent's motives if this is meant to imply a non-causal character to such explanations (*Aspects of Scientific Explanation,* p. 255). Yet we often do speak of explanations of human actions as teleological, and the reason, I believe, is simply that this is a convenient way of calling attention to the importance of goals or ends and of an agent's calculations concerning means to these goals or ends in characteristically human actions.

it thus can provide what I in my interpretation of Hegel have called a fully adequate or complete explanation of this process: "Freedom is itself its own object of attainment and the sole purpose of Spirit. It is the ultimate purpose toward which all world history has continually aimed. . . . Freedom alone is the purpose which realizes and fulfills itself." [42]

Indeed it is freedom which binds together the actions of individual agents pursuing their private interests and the world historical process. Historical men are, however imperfectly, free men deliberately and freely pursuing their own subjective ends, and in the process of doing so they help, unintentionally, to advance the development of freedom in the world historical process. Spirit as self-determining is in need of no explanation beyond this freedom, which is its ultimate end. This, I believe, is why Hegel looked upon all scientific explanations as inferior to the explanation he has provided.

[42] *Reason in History*, p. 25.

Bibliography

Works by G. W. F. Hegel

Hegel's Philosophy of Right. Translated by T. M. Knox. Oxford, 1952.

Hegel's Science of Logic. Translated by A. V. Miller. London, 1969.

Lectures on the History of Philosophy. Translated by E. S. Haldane. London, 1892. Two volumes.

Lectures on the Philosophy of Religion. Translated by E. B. Speirs and J. B. Sanderson. New York, 1962. Two volumes.

The Logic of Hegel. Translated by William Wallace. Oxford, 1892.

The Phenomenology of Mind. Translated by J. B. Baillie. London, 1961.

The Philosophy of History. Translated by J. Sibree. New York, 1944.

The Philosophy of Nature. Translated by A. V. Miller. Oxford, 1970.

Reason in History. Translated by Robert S. Hartman. New York, 1953.

Works by Others

Avineri, Shlomo. "Consciousness and History: *List der Vernunft* in Hegel and Marx," in *New Studies in Hegel's Philosophy*. Edited by W. E. Steinkraus. New York, 1971, pp. 108–118.

Berlin, Isaiah. *Historical Inevitability*. London, 1954.

Canfield, John V., editor. *Purpose in Nature*. Englewood Cliffs, 1966.

Donagan, Alan. *The Later Philosophy of R. G. Collingwood*. Oxford, 1962.

Fain, Haskell. *Between Philosophy and History*. Princeton, 1970.

Findlay, J. N. *Hegel, A Re-examination*. London, 1958.

Hempel, Carl G. *Aspects of Scientific Explanation*. New York, 1965.

Henrich, Dieter. "*Hegels Theorie über den Zufall*," *Kant-Studien*, L (1958–1959), pp. 131–148.

Kaufmann, Walter. *Hegel*. Garden City, 1965.

——. "The Hegel Myth and Its Method," in *Hegel's Political Philosophy*. Edited by Walter Kaufmann. New York, 1970. Pp. 137–171.

MacIntyre, Alasdair. *Herbert Marcuse*. New York, 1970.

Marcus, Ruth B. "Essential Attribution," *The Journal of Philosophy*, LXVIII (April 8, 1971), pp. 187–202.

Marcuse, Herbert. *Reason and Revolution: Hegel and the Rise of Social Theory*. Boston, 1954.

Mueller, Gustav E. "The Hegel Legend of 'Thesis-Antithesis-Synthesis,'" *The Journal of the History of Ideas*, X (June, 1958), pp. 412–414.

Murdoch, Iris. *The Sovereignty of Good*. New York, 1971.

Popper, Karl. *The Open Society and Its Enemies*. Princeton, 1950.

——. *The Poverty of Historicism*. New York, 1961.

Soll, Ivan. *An Introduction to Hegel's Metaphysics*. Chicago, 1969.

Walsh, W. H. "Hegel on the Philosophy of History," *History and Theory* (1965), *Beiheft* V, pp. 67–82.

——. *An Introduction to the Philosophy of History*. London, 1953.

Wilkins, Burleigh T. "Teleology in Kant's Philosophy of History," *History and Theory*, V (1966), pp. 172–185.

Index